BOOMERS!

FUNDING YOUR
FUTURE
IN AN AGE OF
UNCERTAINTY

BY MARK MILLS, CFP, AND NANCY MILLS

PUBLISHING

New York

Editorial Director: Jennifer Farthing
Development Editor: Mary Good
Production Editor: Fred Urfer
Production Artist: Janet Schroeder
Cover Designer: Rod Hernandez

© 2007 by Mark Mills, CFP, and Nancy Mills

Published by Kaplan Publishing,
a division of Kaplan, Inc.

Printed in the United States of America

August 2007

07 08 09 10 9 8 7 6 5 4 3 2 1

ISBN 13: 978-1-4277-5469-1

Kaplan Publishing books are available at special quantity discounts to use for sales promotions, employee premiums, or educational purposes. Please email our Special Sales Department to order or for more information, at kaplanpublishing@kaplan.com, or write to Kaplan Publishing, 1 Liberty Plaza, 24th Floor, New York, NY 10006.

DEDICATION

This book is dedicated to Adam, Tammy, Jacob, Carrie, Grant, and Lauren. You make life worth living, at any age!

Contents

PART FOUR
MONEY

PART FIVE
HEALTH

PART SIX
FAMILY AND COMMUNITY

While the authors have their names on the cover, this book builds upon the work of many, nearly all of them members of Boomer Nation. We especially thank our partner, Bill Charette, who lit the Boomers' path and helped us repeatedly along the way. We thank our colleagues and collaborators, including John Carver, Michael Azevedo, Katie Gulde, Gino Mauro, Ann Peck, Paul Stern, Art Cohen, Gene Mackles, Marty Gardner, and Shady Hartshorne. The insights and enthusiasm of career experts Lin Schreiber and Jeff Williams are most appreciated.

We thank Michael Kolowich for his guidance and technical wizardry, Judy Goggin of Civic Ventures for her friendship and support, and Larry Brink for his wise counsel, generosity, and decades-long friendship.

Our heartfelt admiration goes to John Rosenthal for his support and for setting a high standard for all Boomers. We thank Tom Davison of American Public Television for his encouragement and patience.

We thank the many authors who taught us much and whose work we have quoted, including Fred Brock, Dee Lee, Marc Freedman, and Abigail Trafford.

Much appreciation and thanks go to Mary Good, or Good Mary, whichever you prefer. She is our editor at Kaplan and helped to pull us through the process as first-time authors.

We are Boomers, members of a generation 78 million strong, born in the prosperous postwar years of 1946 to 1964. As members of the older half of the Boomer generation, we shared the good and the bad of many life-shaping experiences. We ducked for cover under school desks in Cold War drills, but eventually saw the Berlin Wall come down. We reveled in the early years of rock 'n' roll, only to see John Lennon gunned down on the streets of New York. While President John F. Kennedy inspired us, his assassination and those of Martin Luther King Jr. and Robert Kennedy were all crushing blows.

Many Boomers protested against the Vietnam War and in favor of civil rights, equal rights, and a cleaner environment. Our distrust of the establishment deepened with the Watergate scandal. We came of age in revolutionary times, a generation hell-bent on challenging authority and changing the world.

Now, as the oldest Boomers enter their early sixties, we are poised to launch a new revolution, reinventing "retirement" and redefining aging in America. With advances in medicine and greater awareness about diet, exercise, and the risks of smoking, many Boomers will make it to age 100. The U.S. Census Bureau estimates that by 2050 there will be nearly one million centenarians. If Willard Scott were still doing the weather on TV, he would have to spend all day congratulating Boomers who were hitting the century mark. For a healthy couple age 65 today, there is a 50 percent chance that at least one of them will live to age 92. That's 27 years past the traditional retirement age of 65. And many will go well beyond that.

Today's Boomers may be around to benefit from remarkable breakthroughs in fields such as stem cell research and nanomedicine, which promise dramatic advances in the diagnosis and treatment of cancer, heart disease, diabetes, and other life-threatening illnesses. Add 20 years of scientific progress, and today's fifty-year-olds may reach 70 with well-founded hopes of enjoying healthy, active lives to 100 and beyond.

Many will use that "longevity bonus" to change careers, start a business, pursue hobbies, get an advanced degree, spend time with family, and give back through civic engagement. Whatever they do, they will not withdraw to the sidelines; they will not slip quietly into later life. Boomers are all about seeking new adventures, experiences, accomplishments, and relationships.

"It's the first time in evolution that we have ever lived so long, so well," says Abigail Trafford, author of *My Time: Making the Most of the Bonus Decades after 50.* "This changes the landscape from sex to politics, to family to work to creativity, and we've only just begun to see what's going to happen in this revolution."

"THE BIG CHURN"

Still, these wonderful prospects are not without risks and worries. Many Boomers are finding themselves in a time of transition. Millions are becoming empty nesters while others are coping with divorce and being single again. Many are still raising children while also caring for elderly parents. "I call it the big churn," says Trafford. "There's a lot of loss. You get to this period in life when doors close, it's absolutely true. There are a lot of problems at this time. You lose your parents, you may suffer in the workplace, your kids go off, and you wonder 'what's next?' But other doors open. The good news is there's potential here. There's potential in relationships, there's potential in work. I have talked to so many people, and they've regenerated, they found new lives and they've said, 'I can't believe it.' But these are really good decades in life."

The setbacks and the opportunities at this time of life make for a mixed blessing, a yin and yang of regret and relief, sadness and joy, optimism and uncertainty. The aim of this book is to inspire Boomers to grab the possibilities, and to offer guidance on navigating the challenges.

NOT YOUR FATHER'S RETIREMENT

Retirement used to be an event: a good-bye party and a gold watch. For most Boomers, fathers were the principal breadwinners. When it was time to retire, our dads usually quit work cold turkey, and began what was billed as a life of leisure, or a permanent vacation. For Boomers, "retirement" will not be an event but a process, an evolving life chapter that lasts for years and includes a mix of paid work, education, volunteering, family activity, travel, and recreation. Eventually, Boomers will adopt a more traditional retirement lifestyle, but at a much later age than did our parents' generation.

This will happen for two main reasons. First, Boomers want to stay in the game, to enjoy the satisfaction, sense of accomplishment, and meaningful relationships that are part of the work experience. Second, they can't afford to quit. This is not a generation of dedicated savers. Growing up during the Great Depression, our parents may have learned to be thrifty. But those lessons didn't transfer to the Boomers, who came of age in affluent postwar America. For both the psychic benefits and financial rewards, Boomers will remain in the workforce in some capacity. They will make it fashionable to keep on truckin', and "uncool" to drop out for a life of bingo and early bird specials.

Studies indicate that 75 to 80 percent of Boomers plan to do some kind of work after age 65. The desire to continue working may vary by occupation. If you work in an office setting, it's not too hard to roll up to the computer for a few years after age 65 to keep reading and writing email. But if you've been cranking away for 30 years in construction or at a meat packing plant, you may not be too eager to keep punching the time clock and pounding away at your body.

But will the economy have room for all these aging Boomers to keep working? Age discrimination has been a serious problem in the American workplace for years. It could become an epidemic with so many older workers in need of a paycheck. But the generation coming up after the Boomers is smaller. It has fewer workers to feed a growing economy. Many employers will need to retain the skills, experience, and solid work habits of the Boomer generation. We may see a happy coinciding of Boomers who want to keep working, and employers who need all the skilled hands they can find.

Work has become less physically demanding, which enables people to stay on the job longer. Most working Boomers are computer literate so they can handle many of today's workplace tasks. They may even be able to telecommute from home, saving employers the cost of office space. The U.S. economy has seen an increase in the use of part-time and temporary workers, which fits neatly into the Boomer desire for part-time employment in "retirement."

More and more, we will find Boomers who consider themselves to be both "retired" and working. Both will be true, but the work will be in a post-career job, probably part-time and hopefully in a field that is personally satisfying.

THE TIMES THEY ARE A-CHANGIN'

While we believe many Boomers will have tremendous opportunities to live exciting and fulfilling lives as they age, we also recognize that we live in uncertain times. Americans face an array of challenges, as a nation and as individuals. From the war on terror to our bulging fiscal deficits, from global competition to global warming, we live in an era fraught with risks and uncertainties.

Ward Cleaver never seemed to worry about job security; today it is a fact of life. Companies are restructuring, shutting down pensions, and forcing workers to pay more for health insurance. We urge people to contribute to their 401(k) plans, but guess what? Now you have to be your own pension fund manager in addition to everything else you do in your life.

We all get annual statements from the federal government detailing our projected Social Security benefits, but Federal Reserve Board Chairman Ben Bernanke calls Medicare and Social Security "unsustainable entitlement programs." To keep them going we have to either cut benefits or raise taxes. President Bush proposed private Social Security accounts. But instead of a guaranteed fixed monthly payment, with private accounts, individuals assume the risk of how their investments perform. Some people would be winners in that system, but there would also be losers.

Traditional social safety nets are less reliable. The old three-legged stool of retirement savings is getting wobbly. As we near the end of our active careers, the system of guaranteed pensions and rock solid Social Security that worked for our parents is fading. We are seeing a transfer of risk, burden, and responsibility from institutions to families and individuals. The reality is we are all much more on our own.

Some Boomers will benefit from an inheritance, but the parents of Boomers are also enjoying increased longevity. They are having a grand time spending their money, as well they should. Many older Americans will require nursing home care, which will rapidly deplete their savings. While Boomers should talk to their parents about estate plans, living wills, and medical proxies, most should not be counting on Mom and Dad to bail them out of their faulty retirement planning.

PULLING OUR WEIGHT

Longer life spans mean we are increasingly a society of four-generation families consisting of Boomers, their children, their grandchildren, and their elderly parents. Young adults and middle-aged workers cannot afford to pay Social Security and Medicare for a leisure class of Boomers, while also footing the bill for educating the young and caring for the truly old and frail. Yet that picture of the greedy Boomer geezer, and its potential for causing intergenerational strife, is a widely held concern. However, Marc Freedman, president of the think tank Civic Ventures, thinks the Boomer generation—which is well educated and highly motivated—will make huge contributions to the greater good. "People who are worried about this vast increase in the older population tell us that the small group of people in the middle are going to be forced to support tens of millions of people older than they are, plus the younger generation, and that there's no way that they're going to be able to stand that increased weight. Well, what about a notion where two generations in the middle band together to support the truly elderly and dependent young people?" In that scenario, Boomers and their adult children will carry the burden of providing care and services to the youngest, oldest, and most vulnerable members of society.

Millions of Boomers will continue working and contributing to the nation's economic vitality and to its tax base. Many will do volunteer work that will assist young and old, and reduce the cost of government-supported social services. As Marc Freedman sees it, "The aging of America is every bit as much an opportunity to be seized as a problem to be solved."

SAVINGS SHORTFALL

Unfortunately, many Boomers do a much better job of planning vacations than they do their own retirements. With so many demands on the household budget, saving can be a last priority, or a lost one. Investing is complicated. Crunching numbers to know how much you'll need in retirement can be daunting. But more daunting is the prospect of being flat broke over your last 30 years. It appears many Boomers will be struggling as they age.

The Boston College Center for Retirement Research estimates that 35 percent of older Boomers (born 1946 to 1954) are at risk of being unable to maintain their preretirement standard of living in retirement. For younger Boomers (born 1955 to 1964), the at-risk figure jumps to 44 percent. The reason for this gloomy outlook, according to the center's 2006 National Retirement Risk Index, is a changing retirement landscape, including an increase in the Social Security retirement age, a sharp decline in traditional pensions, modest 401(k) balances, low savings rates, and longer life spans.

A 2005 study by the Employee Benefit Research Institute (EBRI) looked at the accumulated savings and investments of workers age 45 and older. Here is the woeful scorecard:

Amount Saved*	Ages 45 to 54	Age 55+
• **Less than $25,000:**	41%	39%
• **$25,000–$49,999:**	14%	12%
• **$50,000–$99,999:**	13%	7%
• **$100,000–$249,999:**	17%	23%
• **$250,000 or more:**	16%	19%

* Does not include the value of a primary residence or a traditional company pension.

Note: Percentages may total more than 100 due to the rounding of numbers.

More than half the workers age fifty-five-plus have saved less than $50,000. Eighty-one percent of workers 55 and up have under $250,000. What do these meager savings tallies represent in generating annual income? Let's look at the better-off folks in the quarter-million-dollar club. If you had $250,000, you could withdraw about $13,800 a year for 25 years, increasing the payment by three percent a year for inflation, with the balance in the account growing at an annual rate of six percent. After 25 years, the account is bone dry. That $13,800 plus Social Security doesn't take you very far.

But let's not overstate the downside. The stock market has risen since that 2005 study, and, presumably, most Boomers have continued adding to retirement savings. Traditional pensions and real estate equity, omitted from the EBRI study, will bolster retirement security for millions of people. Moreover, many Boomers will supplement retirement income by continuing to work.

Financial author and public television money expert Jonathan Pond says Boomer prospects are better than most people think. "There is a lot of university and government research which suggests that Boomers are actually in better financial condition than much of the media portray," says Pond. "It doesn't mean they are not challenged, many are. But even the more pessimistic outlooks suggest that 60 to 65 percent are in pretty good shape."

Pond cites a 2006 academic study, "Balance Sheets of Early Boomers: Are They Different from Pre-Boomers?" as an example of the more optimistic research. The report found that Boomers possess a significantly higher level of financial assets than their parents did at the same age. "I wouldn't want people to rest on their laurels," says Pond. "But I wouldn't be discouraged by your prospects because we tend to be inundated with suggestions that we are going to be eating dog food when we retire. But that's not what the really serious and thorough research shows."

CREATE THE FUTURE

Boomers have the chance to be healthy, productive, fulfilled, and happy for many years to come. But we need to plan, save, and prepare. For decades, our generation has been working to build careers, support our families, and meet our obligations. Now, it is time to reconnect with our dreams, to let loose yearnings we have kept in check, and to think about sharing our experience by giving back to the community.

In the coming years, many of us will have more discretion over what to do with our time and how to channel our energy. We can look with anticipation to that promising span of years between the end of a fully engaged career and old age, when options narrow. We need to envision the future we want and then work to make it happen. Some things are beyond our control, but as the late management guru Peter Drucker put it, "The best way to predict the future is to create it."

This book is a guide to shaping the future we want. We offer Boomers the tools to capitalize on what we call "life assets." We present new models for a new stage of life. From changing careers to starting a business, from saving and investing to smart moves in housing, from health care to community service, we offer advice, provide resources, and profile pioneers who are already on the road to a 21st century retirement. These are uncertain times, but we all have the power to create a more positive future for our families and ourselves.

Part One

PLANNING

1

YOU ARE YOUR
BEST ASSET

As you plan the future, make a full assessment of your assets, and we don't mean just the financial kind. We think of assets very broadly. Your accumulated knowledge, skills, experience, and relationships are all assets you can use to shape the future. Your imagination, passion, and determination are more important than your 401(k) balance. Your health is more important than all of the above.

You are an individual with a unique personality. You have a sense of purpose and a sense of humor. You have skills, training, and ambition. You have an education and the capacity to learn much more. You have years of life experience. These are all building blocks for creating the future you desire. Your personal qualities and willingness to expand your horizons will have the biggest impact on shaping a successful transition to retirement.

This chapter is devoted to helping you think about all the assets in your life, to nurture and strengthen those assets and to see how you can use them to achieve your dreams. Here are some ways to do this.

LIFELONG LEARNING

Continue to take courses, read, attend seminars, and seek on-the-job training to expand your knowledge. You can't sit tight on your existing set of skills. The world is changing too fast; you need to keep upgrading. Learn a new software program. Increase your mastery of an existing hobby or take up a new one. These things will keep your mind alert, and can also increase employment opportunities. Knowing how to use a spreadsheet, for example, may help you to land a job or get a worthwhile volunteer assignment. If you can turn a hobby into a part-time business, you may earn income doing something you love.

MAINTAIN YOUR HEALTH

Stay active, be smart about nutrition, and get regular checkups. Too many Americans are sedentary and eat too much of the wrong foods. That's not a good recipe for a long and active life. All the saving we do and all the planning can be negated by failing health. Many illnesses are unavoidable, and we all live with that risk. But too many health problems are self-inflicted. Smoking, alcohol abuse, high-fat diets, and physical inactivity can contribute to cancer, heart disease, and diabetes.

The *New York Times* reported that life insurance premiums for overweight people are two to four times more than for individuals with normal weight. The report said overweight people "can expect higher medical expenses, and they tend to make less money and accumulate less wealth in their shortened lifetimes. They can have a harder time being hired, and then a harder time winning plum assignments and promotions." Something to think about next time you order a donut with your morning coffee.

Just as listing assets and liabilities takes a snapshot of your financial health, numbers such as blood pressure and cholesterol readings give a picture of your physical health. For Boomers, getting regular checkups is an essential part of good health. Catching a problem early can save your life. By taking regular readings of blood pressure and cholesterol levels, your doctor can advise you on preventative steps before problems arise. You can learn more about these numbers at www.webmd.com.

Working past age 65 or starting a business takes energy, and being fit keeps up stamina. Beyond employment, a healthy body is crucial to fulfilling many of our retirement dreams. If playing golf at Pebble Beach, climbing Mt. Rainier, dancing the night away in Paris, or just keeping up with your grandchildren is part of your retirement vision, invest in your health. Make the time to take care of yourself. It is never too late to start.

Measuring Up

Body mass index, or BMI, is one health indicator you can calculate on your own. It is a measure of body fat based on height and weight that applies to both adult men and women. To calculate your BMI you divide your weight in pounds by the square of your height in inches, and multiply that number by 703 (for metric conversion purposes). Then check your BMI against this scale to see where you stand:

Underweight = <18.5

Normal weight = 18.5–24.9

Overweight = 25–29.9

Obese = BMI of 30 or greater

Examples:

A man 5' 11" weighing 190 lb: **190/ (71 × 71) × 703 = 26.5**

(Overweight)

A woman 5' 4" weighing 132 lb: **132/ (64 × 64) × 703 = 22.7**

(Normal weight)

Critics claim the index is not accurate for very muscular people, but for most of us, it can provide a needed wake-up call. If all this math has your eyes glazing over, the National Heart, Lung, and Blood Institute, a federal agency, has a BMI calculator at www.nhlbisupport.com/bmi.

NURTURE RELATIONSHIPS

Satisfying long-term relationships are a key to happiness. Relationships with spouses, partners, children, and friends are like gardens; they need care and tending, and patience, too. But they are beautiful and enrich our lives.

Research shows that married people tend to live longer, be happier, and have more wealth and better sex lives than the single or divorced. A Centers for Disease Control study found that regardless of age, sex, race, education, or income, married adults were generally healthier than adults in other marital status categories. One exception was married adults, particularly men, who were overweight or obese compared to the unmarried. ("Marital Status and Health: United States, 1999–2002," December 2004).

Maintaining friendships leads to more satisfaction as we age. Close friends are there to celebrate the good times and provide caring support in the hard times. They give us advice and help to keep us on track, and we do the same in return. A supportive network of friendships can extend longevity and increase happiness. In a highly mobile society, with job changes and moving, most of us have lost touch with past friends. But cultivating long-term friendships as a network of social support can be a vital ingredient in a satisfying midlife and retirement.

Professional relationships are also an asset for Boomers. Most of us have been in our careers for many years, and may have hundreds of colleagues and associates, past and present. Those connections can be a big plus if you suddenly lose your job, or if you want to start a business, or help a son or daughter get a job interview. Maintain your network of contacts. Keep participating in professional associations. Staying in touch with people is both satisfying and useful in forging the next phase of your life.

THE JOYS OF WORK

Your job is an asset that provides much more than a paycheck. Work is the source of a wide array of personal, financial, and social benefits for millions of American households. Some benefits meet our immediate needs, and some can help us to achieve our future goals. The list of benefits includes the following:

- Job training
- Health insurance
- Life and disability insurance
- Pensions
- Social Security
- Vacations and holidays
- Sick leave
- Education reimbursement
- Flexible spending accounts
- Family leave policies
- Workers' compensation
- Unemployment insurance
- Employee discounts

On the personal side, work is a great place to make friends or meet a potential spouse. It is where we can bond with a team, yet find personal pride and satisfaction. All told, work is a vital asset in our lives. If a job is lost, it cuts deeply in many ways.

Starting with our paychecks, we depend on many of these benefits in the near term—bills to pay this month, a sick day next week, a vacation next summer. However, some benefits have longer-term value, and Boomers should take full advantage of these while they are available.

401(k) Plans and Pensions

The 401(k) plan is the most critical long-term asset at work. About 83 percent of Boomers who have a 401(k) available participate in the plans. But that means one in six does not. Many of those who do participate do not contribute enough to their accounts. People are reluctant to lower their take-home pay by saving for retirement, a choice they may regret if they have to keep working well into their seventies. The best way to save is to "pay yourself first." Yes, we know you have heard that old adage a million times, but the reason it has been around so long is that it works. And these days, it works better than ever. With direct deposit and automatic investment programs, you can set up an investing plan and make it all happen like clockwork.

The 401(k) builds this right in. Contributions go into your account automatically, before you have a chance to get your hands on the money. Try to push yourself to contribute more to your 401(k) than you have been. Save an additional $200 a month for the next 10 years, earning eight percent annually, and you will accumulate an extra $36,000. That alone would yield $250 a month in income for the following 25 years. You may think you can't save $200 more a month, but you may be surprised at how easily you survive when you never see the cash.

If you have a 401(k) or similar plan, you are always entitled to keep the contributions you make to the plan. But if your employer makes matching contributions, plan rules may require a certain length of employment before those matching dollars are yours to keep. If you plan to leave your job, don't quit two weeks before locking in the matching funds.

If your employer offers a traditional pension, known as a defined benefit plan, think long and hard before leaving that job for greener pastures. Employers are solely responsible for funding and managing these plans. Once you retire, a defined benefit plan provides either a lump sum payment or a monthly check for the rest of your life. That payment is based on your salary and length of service. If you have a defined benefit pension and are thinking of leaving your job, include the value of the pension in weighing your employment options. These types of pensions are fast disappearing from the American workplace. Even if you find another job with a defined benefit plan, the plans are structured to reward seniority, not job-hopping. If you are leaving a job and can control the timing of your departure, make sure you do not leave just before being credited with one more year on the job, which would boost your monthly pension payment in retirement.

Later in the book, we devote a chapter to the basics of investing, a chapter to mastering your 401(k), and another to IRAs, annuities, and other retirement savings tools.

Measuring Up

Here is an example of how length of service at a company can greatly enhance a defined benefit pension. Pay level and the number of years on the job determine the lump sum value or monthly payment from a pension. The formula for determining the pension might work this way: **average annual pay for last 5 years × 1.5 percent × number of years on the job.**

A worker with 15 years of service who averaged $60,000 a year over the last 5 years of work would receive the following:

$60,000 × .015 × 15 = $13,500 per year, or $1,125 per month

If the employee continued working another 5 years and received a 3 percent pay raise each year, the pension would rise considerably:

$65,620 × .015 × 20 = $19,686 per year, or $1,640 per month

The last 5 years of employment represent just one-quarter of the worker's total years of service, but the pension is 46 percent higher than if the employee had left 5 years earlier.

Benefits would be lower if the worker chooses a "joint and survivor" payment, in which a surviving spouse continues to receive a pension after the retiree's death.

Health and Life Insurance

If you are laid off or leave your job and do not have access to another health insurance plan, you may be entitled by law to purchase health insurance through your old employer's group plan for up to 18 months. This benefit is available under COBRA, the Consolidated Omnibus Budget Reconciliation Act of 1986. It applies to companies with 20 or more employees.

Paying for health insurance under COBRA is not cheap; the company no longer provides the subsidy you received as an employee. But at least you can purchase the insurance at the group rate, plus a two percent administrative charge. While this premium may give you sticker shock, it will likely be hundreds of dollars per month less than buying a comparable policy in the open market.

If a child is covered by your plan while attending college, after graduation he or she may lose his or her dependent status. But dependents who lose coverage are also entitled to COBRA benefits. You can purchase their health insurance through your employer (and then hope that your son or daughter quickly gets a job with full benefits!). Consult your HR department for details on how and when to make the switch from your coverage to the COBRA plan.

COBRA offers another protection. By federal law, if you go for a period of 63 days or more without health insurance coverage, when you eventually join another group plan, the insurer can refuse to cover treatment of a preexisting condition for up to 12 months. With continuous health insurance coverage, available through COBRA, you avoid a break in coverage, so that when you join another plan your preexisting condition is covered. Going without health insurance is risky for any Boomer, but this little known preexisting condition exclusion is another good reason to avoid any gaps in coverage.

Many life insurance plans offered at work allow you to buy extra insurance, over the amount you receive as a company benefit. Usually this insurance costs more than what a healthy person would pay in the open market. In part, that is because these plans generally do not require a physical examination. In return for taking on the risk of selling policies to all employees regardless of health, insurance companies charge a higher premium. If you are healthy and want extra life insurance, you will do better buying it on your own. But if you have health issues that would bar you from qualifying for life insurance in the open market, consider getting extra insurance through your employer. Make sure you can keep the policy if you leave your job.

Be Flexible

If your employer offers a "flexible spending account," consider signing up. These accounts allow workers to set aside pretax dollars for dependent care and out-of-pocket medical expenses. The dependent care accounts are used mostly for child day care, but can also apply to day care expenses for an elder parent. To use this program for elder care, you must provide at least half of a parent's financial support.

The medical accounts let you use tax-free dollars to pay for expenses not covered by health insurance. These include deductibles and co-payments, eyeglasses, dental care, and many prescription and over-the-counter medications. Flex account enrollment generally takes place late in the year, to take effect the following year. If you think that next year you will need some new glasses and have some dental crown work done, you can estimate those costs and pay them off with tax-free dollars.

Contributions are deducted from your paycheck and held in a special account. After paying for qualified expenses, you are reimbursed with your own tax-free dollars. Flex account contributions are exempt from federal and most state income taxes, and FICA taxes, so the savings can be considerable. One hitch: If you set aside more money than you end up using, you forfeit the unused dollars. Only set aside what you are certain you will use.

Hit the Books

Many Boomers underutilize the education reimbursement benefit. Getting your employer to pay for additional education can help you to learn new skills, which can increase your job security or help you prepare for a career change. While these plans generally require that courses relate to your job, you can probably make a convincing case to take many courses that match your goals and ambitions. If you are thinking of starting your own business someday, tell your boss how useful it would be for you to take an accounting course so you will better understand those dreaded budget meetings. Remember, once you learn something it is yours forever (or at least until you forget it)!

INVESTMENTS

Your investments are a major life-planning asset, and Boomers need to keep building up their accounts and making sure their hard-earned dollars are invested wisely. One challenge for experienced workers is that they may have several different retirement accounts, from old 401(k)s to IRAs to annuities. A spouse or partner may have several more accounts. It can become a confusing patchwork, even though all the accounts exist for the same purpose: your retirement nest egg.

You may be able to consolidate some of the accounts by combining IRAs or transferring an old 401(k) into a rollover IRA. More important, Boomers need to look at the big picture, to take a holistic view to make sure these accounts are working in a coordinated fashion. Unless you map out all your retirement investments to see which areas should be bolstered, you will not know the best way to invest future 401(k) contributions.

ASSETS FROM UNCLE SAM

Social Security is not just a government benefit; it is an asset, earned by years of hard work. However, it is not guaranteed. The federal government can change the program, and has done so many times over the years. Many observers think the current system is unsustainable, and that benefits will have to be cut, taxes increased, or some combination of the two.

For years, the Social Security program has taken in more than it pays out. The government spends the surplus on other programs and gives Social Security IOUs, which go into trust funds to be tapped when current revenue can no longer fully fund the program. No actual money exists in the trust funds, so the government will have to borrow more to pay off those IOUs.

In 2006, the Social Security Board of Trustees estimated that payroll tax revenue will fall below the cost of benefits in 2017, and that the trust funds will be exhausted in 2040. In 2040, the oldest Boomers will be 94; the youngest will be 76. The system will still be facing heavy obligations at a time when its reserves are gone and its revenue is insufficient.

At some point, the federal government will have to address the problem. Cutting benefits and raising taxes are both unpopular solutions. Proposals to establish private accounts have been criticized as too risky for individual workers. Meanwhile, the time bomb keeps ticking.

Will You Get Yours?

From a planning perspective, we think the older half of Boomer Nation is likely to get most, if not all, of the currently scheduled benefits. If payroll taxes increase, it will impact younger Boomers more because they have more years of work ahead of them. Income taxes on Social Security benefits will affect more people over time. For couples, benefits are taxable if the total of half your Social Security plus your other income exceeds $32,000. For singles the limit is $25,000. For this test, total income includes interest from tax-exempt bonds. Because these tax thresholds have not changed in more than 20 years, more people are hitting the trip wire every April 15. It's a backdoor tax on retirees that, in effect, reduces Social Security benefits. Had those income limits been indexed to inflation since they took effect in 1984, taxes would kick in today at $62,000 for couples and $48,000 for singles. It is no accident that those limits haven't budged since Ronald Reagan signed them into law in 1983.

One reform passed in the 1983 legislation stipulates gradual increases for receiving full Social Security benefits from ages 65 to 67. The change phases in, depending on the year of your birth. For Boomers born between 1946 and 1954, full retirement age is 66. For those born in 1955, full retirement age is 66 and 2 months; this gradually rises to 66 and 10 months for those born in 1959. Starting with births in 1960, the full retirement age is 67. While this appears to be a benefit cut, increased longevity means many Boomers will receive a larger lifetime payout than prior generations, even if they wait until 66 or 67 to start receiving payments.

Despite this change, Boomers can still elect to start receiving Social Security at age 62. Those taking payments before reaching the full retirement age receive a permanently reduced benefit. Our chapter "Retirement Savings Toolbox" examines the pros and cons of taking early benefits.

What Is Social Security Worth?

One way to place a value on Social Security as an asset is to determine how much of a lump sum in cash would be needed to replicate the monthly payment Social Security provides. Here is an example of one calculation, starting with some assumptions:

- You will collect Social Security for 25 years, from age 66 to age 91.
- Your monthly payment is $1,250, or $15,000 a year.
- Payments increase each year by three percent to keep up with inflation.
- Account balance earns six percent a year.

The lump sum you would need to generate $15,000 a year with the above assumptions is $263,758. All those FICA deductions over the years actually meant something. If you die, your heirs won't collect that big stash. But a surviving spouse can continue to receive the full benefit, if he or she is of retirement age. Your circumstances will vary from this example, but it illustrates the value of Social Security as an asset.

Medicare

Medicare is national health insurance for people age 65 and over. With the growing number of older Americans, longer life spans, and rising health care costs, the Medicare system is also under financial stress. The 2006 report of the Medicare Board of Trustees said, "Medicare's financial difficulties come sooner—and are much more severe—than those confronting Social Security."

Of your total FICA tax, 6.2 percent goes into the retirement side (which also covers survivor and disability benefits), and 1.45 percent is earmarked for Medicare. Employers match those payments dollar for dollar. But as health care costs spiral out of control, the pressure to raise the Medicare portion of the FICA tax will grow. Reforms may also cut benefits or impose fees on more affluent participants.

We focus on Medicare in a later chapter on health insurance. But one fact stands out in our research: Despite Medicare's benefits, there are many gaps in coverage, and medical expenses for older Americans remain quite high. We can count Medicare as an asset, but we still have to set aside significant funds to cover the cost of health care.

PROPERTY, PLANT, AND EQUIPMENT

Property, plant, and equipment, or PP&E, is an accounting term for tangible assets owned by a business or other organization. From land to houses, from cars to computers, most Boomers also have significant PP&E items on our balance sheets. Some of these assets can play a key role in preparing for the future.

A house provides shelter. It is where we raise our families, celebrate our victories, cry over losses, and make a lifetime of memories. In addition to all of these things, a home is an important financial asset. While some parts of the country have not had significant appreciation in housing prices, other areas, especially near the East and West Coasts, have seen tremendous gains in home values. Many Boomers will be selling property at a profit and using the cash to generate income in the next phase of their lives.

Like most investments, real estate can be fickle. Though price swings are not as volatile as in the stock market, housing markets have up and down cycles, too. Some analysts say that with fewer young people coming along after the Boomers, demand for housing may eventually slow, and prices may go flat or even retreat. No one knows for sure what will happen, but some Boomers have already cashed out of their four-bedroom suburban houses and downsized to a condo or moved to a lower-cost area.

Just as a business must maintain its PP&E, home owners should maintain their property to get maximum value when it is time to sell. Leaking gutters, rotting trim, wet basements, insect damage—all of these, and an endless list of other horrors, can cost a seller thousands of dollars. Like all the assets we have described, our homes need attention and care. A well-kept house is a pleasure to live in, and is much easier to sell when you are ready to move on. Because it is such a critical subject for Boomers, two chapters of this book are devoted to housing options and the financial considerations of real estate.

TIME ON OUR SIDE

Aside from our health and our relationships, time may be the most precious Boomer asset. The older we get, the more we appreciate its value. The good news is we can expect many more years in which to make the most of our time. But there are no guarantees, so there is no time to waste.

After long careers and many years of raising families, millions of Boomers are feeling like now is *their* time. In the coming years, millions more will enter the same phase. It is time to reconnect with dreams and rediscover old ambitions. It is time to book the trips not taken and read the books we had no time to open. It may be time to rekindle an old romance or refinish an old chest of drawers.

Options are opening up. There are plans to be made, goals to be met, times to be had. They say time is money. But you can spend money and make more. Once you've spent time, it is gone forever. Time is the gift. Like all of our assets, let's use it wisely.

2

HERE TODAY,
WHERE TOMORROW?

Our children go to school some 16 years to prepare for careers that last about 40 years. How much time do Boomers spend preparing for the post-career life stage that might last 30 years or more? Yes, our children are learning things that will last a lifetime, but the point is most of us need to spend more time and thought on what we will do after our primary careers have ended.

We need to ask ourselves, and possibly our mates, many probing questions about the future, including the following:

- Do we want to work after "retirement"?
- Will it be part-time work, a career change, a new business?
- Where do we want to live?
- What lifestyle do we want?
- Do we plan to travel?
- Is volunteering in the community a priority?
- Do we need to care for elderly parents?
- Will we receive an inheritance?

- Do our children or grandchildren need financial help or direct care?
- Do we want to leave an estate?
- If we stop full-time work before age 65, what health care options are available?
- What have I always wanted to do, but never had the chance?

Underlying all of this is the question of money. Will you have the financial resources to accomplish the goals you set? Your plans and your assets have to match. If they are out of synch, you must alter your plans or build up your assets, or do some of each.

Many Boomers are still fully engaged in raising families and building careers. Some are getting closer to the point when they can follow their passions and explore new avenues. Whatever your circumstances, it is not too early to envision the future, to start asking questions about what you want to do, and to begin filling in the answers.

Boomers can expect to live longer than past generations, so planning has to cover a longer span of time. The post-career years may encompass several very different stages, from an energetic period of part-time work and volunteering, to an active phase of recreation and travel, to a tranquil time of hobbies and family activities, evolving into the quiet routines of old age. It is a lot more enticing to think about those first 15 to 20 years when we not only have more free time, but plenty of energy to make the journey an exciting and rewarding one.

MAKE YOUR OWN BLUEPRINT

Good life planning is specific. That means a time, a place, an action, and, often, a financial component. The following are examples of life goals:

- I want to retire in 10 years, downsize to a condo, and live on $60,000 a year.
- I want to get a teaching certificate and be teaching social studies in three years.
- I want to sell my house in six years and move to a rural area with nearby golf and skiing.
- When I'm 67, I want to spend a year living in France and learning to cook.
- I want to work part-time in an academic setting for the next five years.
- I am saving $5,000 a year to start a new business when I am 62.
- This year I want to do volunteer work involving young people and sports.
- I want to get involved in community theatre next summer.

These are all reasonable goals for Boomers, and the kinds of things many people are planning to do. Setting that goal is a great starting point. If you are married or have a partner, you need to share your respective dreams and see how well they match. If there are conflicts, look for ways to satisfy both your needs. That means realizing your partner may do some things independently, such as take a trip, teach a course, or build a house with Habitat for Humanity.

We know of couples whose visions of the future clash. Sometimes age is a factor. One person is in retirement mode, and the other, a few years younger, is geared up for a few more years in a high-powered career. Both goals are legitimate, and both should be accommodated. That requires open communication, mutual respect, and willingness to negotiate.

Goals need to be realistic. If you want to retire in 10 years and live on $75,000 a year, you have to make sure the numbers add up. If your savings, 401(k), and Social Security will only give you $60,000 a year, you may need to adjust your goals, or determine how much extra money to save in the next 10 years to hit your target.

Crunching the Numbers

How much should you save for retirement? A key factor is how much you can withdraw from your savings during retirement. Here is a calculation for how much $100,000 can generate in annual income. You can multiply the result of the calculation by the number of hundred thousands you expect to have. We'll use the following assumptions:

- The account earns an average of six percent a year during retirement.
- The savings will support you for 25 years.
- Payments go up each year by three percent to keep pace with inflation.

Your first annual withdrawal is $5,526. Because of inflation, the payment in year 25 is $11,233. After that, the balance is zero. If you have $500,000 in savings, your annual take is five times $5,526, or $27,630. If you make it to the millionaires' club, you can squeeze out $55,260. If your investment returns are better or worse than six percent, you will generate more or less than the numbers shown here.

Beyond that, most people have Social Security, and, hopefully, some other savings. Fortunate Boomers may also have a pension. Add it all up and you can estimate retirement income. If the numbers look too low, you should save more for retirement, or possibly work beyond normal retirement age. That gives you more years to build up savings, and fewer years for taking withdrawals from your account.

AND THE NUMBER IS . . .

A long simmering debate in the field of personal finance revolves around how much money people need to live on in retirement. One widely accepted rule of thumb is that you need 70 to 80 percent of your preretirement income to maintain your standard of living in retirement. That means if household income in your last year of work is $100,000, you will need retirement income of $70,000 to $80,000 a year.

We attended a financial seminar given by a major mutual fund company at which the speaker said some people need more than 100 percent of their preretirement income to satisfy pent-up appetites for travel and recreation during the first few years of retirement. That suggestion got the attention of the mostly affluent audience, but setting such a high standard may be a disservice. Most people could never save enough to meet that target, and in feeling they have failed, may view their retirement prospects with despair. Boomers need to set realistic goals, and they need encouragement to plan and save to meet those goals.

Some financial experts offer a more heartening view. Former *New York Times* business writer Fred Brock says people can get by on about half their preretirement income. Brock has a full bag of tricks on how to live on less in retirement, from moving to a lower cost area and driving a used car to saving on clothing, commuting, and meals out (more on Brock's formula in chapter 6).

Getting by on 80 percent of preretirement income is practically built in to retirement. If you are saving 10 percent of income in your final year of work, you are living on just 90 percent of your pay. FICA taxes of 7.65 percent are taken out of employment income (up to an annual limit); Social Security, pensions, and investment income are not subject to FICA. That's more money you were earning but not receiving. In addition, if income declines by 20 percent, income taxes will drop. From those three sources alone (retirement savings, FICA, lower income tax), gross income can shrink by 20 percent, without reducing take-home pay by a penny. Whatever expenses you can cut will further lower the level of preretirement income you need in the post-career years.

On this issue of "the number," we give a thumbs down to the old rules of thumb. Boomers will go through multiple phases in "retirement." Spending in some years will be higher than in others. In the early years, employment income may reduce the need to dip into savings.

Boomer Optimist

Aging and life planning expert James Weil says many Boomers are far too pessimistic about retirement, and that they are stuck in an old way of thinking. "The great majority of Boomers in my experience don't have a clear new model," says Weil. "They don't have a view of the world as it can be for them. They are stuck, unfortunately, with the old cultural values, the old cultural norms, and the old way of looking at things. Most of them still think that it's about the money, that they don't have enough, and that they are going to have to continue to work, and that work is bad."

Weil tackles that old thinking head on. While many Boomers have not saved enough to match the ideal models of the investment industry's charts and graphs, Weil says many people can live happily on less. "They don't need 70 or 80 or 90 percent of their (pre-retirement) income in order to be happy. They don't, and it's been proven over and over again. There are lots of people who are not living on 70 percent of what they used to earn."

A widely respected authority in the field of successful aging, Weil urges less focus on number crunching and more on composing the life we want. "The new way to look at it is that it's not about your money, it's about your life. You've got a third of your life ahead of you. Most, if not all, of that is going to be in good health. So the real question is, 'What am I going to do? What is it that is going to allow my passions to come out, where I can contribute to the world, contribute to the community?'"

Boomers won't have to retire cold turkey. They can "retire" from a primary career, says Weil, and then supplement income by working in jobs that turn them on. Find an outlet for a passion and make a little extra money at it. Maybe you love golf. OK, so you can't make it on the Champions Tour. But you might get a job managing a club or assisting in the pro shop. Earning extra income in a field you enjoy will stretch your retirement savings, and maybe you can sneak in some free golf in the off-hours. Do you love art? Work part-time in a museum. Fancy yourself as a gourmet cook? Put your skills to work in a restaurant kitchen. Are you interested in helping others? Become a coach, teacher, or tutor.

(continued)

B o o m e r   O p t i m i s t *(continued)*

These may all be lower paying jobs than you have had. But you would not be building a career at this stage; rather you are just finding something you enjoy doing that brings in extra money. "The new way of looking at work is that you get to do what you love to do," says Weil. "What are my passions? What are my hobbies? What are the things that give me energy? And then you say, how do I work in that particular field or that particular industry, so that when you get up and go to 'work' every day, you are doing your life's work. You are doing what you love to do, not what you have to do, and you can get paid for it."

As more Boomers reach traditional retirement age, Weil sees big changes coming. "What absolutely is going to happen in this country is that a major shift will take place," he says. "It's going to be gradual; it's not going to happen overnight. But five years from now retirement planning as we know it will be totally different. It will be much more about life planning first, and financial planning second. Employers will begin to adapt and we'll be looking at a totally different world. It's very exciting."

Boomers will tighten their belts one year to spend more the next. Paying off a mortgage lowers overhead. For some, living costs can be cut in innovative ways through cohousing and group purchases of goods and services. Hard and fast rules will not fit the Boomer contingent. They will figure out a way to make it work, but it won't be as pretty or predictable as those glossy brochures sent out by the mutual fund companies.

THE INFLATION FACTOR

The Boomer life plan should take into account the corrosive effects of inflation. We have been fortunate in recent years to see relatively tame inflation, but many Boomers remember a more unsettling time. The first oil embargo struck in 1973. As gas lines lengthened, oil prices shot up, and inflation averaged 8.7 percent from 1973 to 1983, peaking at 13.3 percent in 1979. Over the last 75 years, inflation has averaged around three percent, and we have been slightly under that in the past two decades.

Even a seemingly benign inflation rate of three percent whittles away purchasing power, like an endless drip of water that wears down granite rock. At three percent inflation, the value of a dollar is cut in half in 24 years. And some critical areas, such as health care, are going up at a much higher rate. Social Security is indexed to inflation; most pensions are not. When calculating what you can take out of savings and retirement accounts, be sure to include an inflation factor, as we did in the "Crunching the Numbers" section of this chapter. Many mutual fund company websites have retirement calculators, as does the website www.fincalc.com. If you want to see the historical impact of inflation, visit the website www.westegg.com/inflation. Type in any two years between 1800 and 2006 and see what happened to prices during that period.

DEBT IS A FOUR-LETTER WORD

With attitudes shaped by the Depression and World War II, the parents of Boomers had conservative views about spending, saving, and borrowing. Unfortunately, most Boomers did not inherit the saving gene. Easy credit, home equity loans, and a mortgage refinancing frenzy have encouraged Boomers to borrow more and keep on spending. Too many people age 50 and older are still racking up credit card debt and getting into trouble. Increasingly, America's safety net is made of plastic. During the 1990s, the average American family racked up a 53 percent increase in credit card debt. But Americans 65 and older swiped their cards at a more furious pace, increasing credit card debt by 149 percent, according to AARP Public Policy Institute. AARP reports that in 2003 "there were 1.6 million [bankruptcy] filings, double the number from a decade before. Many filers were age 50 and older."

Boomers should be paying down debt, not taking on more. Increasing debt means borrowing against future income to pay for current consumption. But most of us are going to need that future income to cover living expenses; carrying a load of consumer debt into retirement is baggage we do not need. Whipping out the plastic to spend money you don't have for things you don't need is dangerous to your financial health and your long-term security.

PLANNING WITH A PRO

Deciding on what you want to do in retirement and where you want to live are key issues in planning the future. But developing a financial plan to support your goals can be complicated. You may need a financial planner to tackle questions such as the following:

- How much money do you need to accumulate to achieve your retirement goals?
- How much do you need to save each month to reach your target?
- What investments are likely to achieve your required rate of return?
- How can you minimize taxes?
- What is the best way to withdraw money during retirement?

A qualified planner can help you answer these and many other critical questions on the road to retirement. Choosing a planner is a very personal decision. You want someone who is competent, honest, experienced in the kind of planning you need, transparent about fees, and someone who listens well, shows empathy, and makes you feel comfortable.

Clients share a considerable amount of private information with a planner, and not just financial information. Medical issues, children's special needs, family conflicts, and personal dreams and fears can all come out in discussing a financial plan. It takes a trusting relationship to produce an effective plan. Many financial planners will provide a complimentary initial meeting to see if it's a good fit for both parties. The Financial Planning Association (FPA), an industry trade group, recommends that clients interview three planners before making a choice.

Planners should provide prospective clients with a Form ADV, or its equivalent. That's a brochure, required by state and federal regulators, in which planners provide considerable information about themselves and their practices.

What to Ask

Many people call themselves financial planners, but some are more interested in selling you products than in planning your future. One highly regarded industry credential is the Certified Financial Planner (CFP) designation. CFPs have taken numerous courses, passed a rigorous examination, pledged to follow ethical guidelines, and must earn continuing education credits. The FPA recommends that clients ask prospective planners about these areas:

- Financial planning and other financial designations the planner holds
- Educational background and work experience
- Licenses to sell certain financial products, such as life insurance or securities
- Services the planner provides
- The planner's basic approach to financial planning
- Types of clients the planner serves, and any minimum net worth or income requirements
- How the planner prepares a plan
- How the planner might address your particular needs
- Whether the planner or others will implement recommendations from the plan

- Business relationships the planner has that might present a conflict of interest
- How the planner is paid for services and the typical charges

If you are thinking about changing careers or starting a business, a financial planner can help you analyze the financial implications of your decision. That may include issues around pensions or health care insurance, or generating enough income to carry you through the transition.

In addition to crunching numbers and developing an investment portfolio, a financial planner can provide guidance on long-term care insurance, taxes, college funding, real estate transactions, charitable giving, estate planning, and other areas.

How Planners Are Paid

Fee-only. The planner is compensated entirely from fees for purposes of consultation, plan development, or investment management. These fees may be charged on an hourly or project basis depending on your needs, or on a percentage of assets under management.

Commission-only. There is no charge for the planner's advice or preparation of a financial plan. Compensation is received solely from the sale of financial products you agree to purchase in order to implement financial planning recommendations.

Combination Fee/Commission. A fee is charged for consultation, advice, and financial plan preparation on an hourly, project, or percentage basis. In addition, the planner may receive commissions from the sale of recommended products used to implement your plan.

Fee-offset. Commissions from the sale of financial products are offset against fees charged for the planning process.

Salary. Some planners work on a salary and bonus basis for financial services firms.

Source: Financial Planning Association

THE NOT-SO-ALMIGHTY DOLLAR

So much of retirement planning focuses on finances. We like to say, "It's not about your money; it's about your life." Doing what you want to do, living the life you desire is what's important. You may be able to simplify your life, and find more happiness with less money.

Nationally recognized as the father of the life planning movement, George Kinder is the founder of the Kinder Institute of Life Planning. A practicing financial planner and tax advisor for nearly 30 years, Kinder is the author of *The Seven Stages of Money Maturity: Understanding the Spirit and Value of Money in Your Life*. It is considered by many to be the seminal work in the burgeoning field of life planning. Here are some of his thoughts on creating a fulfilling life, and keeping money in perspective:

"The process of life planning itself pulls the clients away from living a much more materialistic life, and toward a life that is more filled with spirit and who they are, and who they want to be. The simplest way to describe what a life planner does is to describe three questions that a life planner will typically ask a client. The first question is if you had all the money that you needed, how would you live your life, how would you change your life? The second question goes a little deeper, and that question is if you suddenly discovered that you only had five or ten years left to live, what would you do differently with your life? The third question goes to the deepest place of all for most clients, and that question is if you go to the doctor and the doctor says, 'I'm sorry but you only have 24 hours left to live,' and this takes you totally by surprise, what did you miss, who did you not get to be, what did you not get to do?

"That question really hits bedrock with people. And it is in the answer to that question that the life plan is born. These are the questions that we form a financial plan around rather than the traditional question of when do you want to retire, where do you want your home or your second home to be, how are you going to educate your kids? The focus is really much deeper than that. What is it that is going to bring a person into fruition in life, bring them alive, make them vital again? The reason baby Boomers would come in the first time and say, 'I can't do anything I've dreamed of doing,' is because they're thinking of life as just a bunch of numbers, and they haven't lived up to what those numbers somehow meant to them. Often what we are doing is looking at simplifying how they are spending their time, or simplifying how they are spending their money. And that is nearly always possible."

Part Two

WORK

3

WORKPLACE
REVOLUTION

Many Boomers remember the beatnik character Maynard G. Krebs on the *Dobie Gillis* TV show. Played by the late actor Bob Denver, Maynard G. Krebs shuddered and blurted out the word "work" in a high-pitched voice at the mere suggestion of having to do any work. For Maynard G., work was the ultimate four-letter word. Boomers have been just the opposite. They have been a career-oriented generation, most of whom plan to remain in the workforce beyond the age when previous generations have called it quits.

"The baby Boomers have an identity with their jobs that their parents never had," says former *New York Times* financial columnist Fred Brock. "Baby Boomers don't think of themselves as having jobs, they think of themselves as having careers. They are professionals. It's a part of their psyche; it's a part of their emotional makeup. They can't just walk away from that. They are going to retire, but they are going to transition to some other kind of lifestyle that involves working, but on their own terms."

Numerous surveys show that a large majority of Boomers intend to keep working past age 65. Many will need to work for financial reasons or to maintain health benefits; some want to keep working for personal satisfaction. Since Boomers are going to live longer and be healthier than past generations, it makes sense to keep working to a later age. Retirement at age 65 is rapidly becoming an outmoded concept. As the oldest Boomers approach their mid-sixties, many have so much knowledge, experience, and energy that dropping out of the workforce would be a huge loss, both for individuals and for society.

One of the most widely cited studies of Boomers and work, conducted by AARP in 2003, shows that 79 percent of Boomers plan to work in some capacity during their "retirement" years. Preferences broke down as follows:

- 30 percent plan to work part-time for enjoyment's sake.
- 25 percent plan to work part-time for the needed income.
- 15 percent, more than one in seven, plan to start a business.
- 7 percent plan to change careers but work full-time.
- 20 percent do not want to work beyond age 65.
- 3 percent other.

PURPOSE AND A PAYCHECK

If Boomers follow through on their intentions to work into their late sixties and beyond, it will mean revolutionary change in the workplace. In a 2006 Pew Research Center study, only 12 percent of current retirees said that they were working either full-time or part-time. An Employee Benefit Research Institute survey found that just 27 percent of retirees have ever worked for pay after retirement. That compares to nearly four out of five Boomers who say they intend to keep working. While some Boomers are likely to change their minds about future work, and some will be sidelined by health problems, a major workforce trend is emerging.

Experts cite many reasons for the shift. Longer life spans mean more years of relying on retirement savings. Working beyond 65 extends the time for building up a retirement nest egg. Declines in traditional pensions and retiree health care benefits also encourage workers to keep punching the clock. Work is less physically strenuous than in the past, allowing people to stay productive longer. The social benefits of employment are also a major incentive to keep working. From on-the-job friendships, to building self-esteem, to keeping an active mind and body, Boomers have many reasons to stay engaged and continue contributing beyond the traditional retirement age.

Staying on the job longer means higher income once you do retire, according to Jonathan Pond, author of *You Can Do It! The Boomer's Guide to a Great Retirement*. "The fact that [Boomers] want to retire later rather than sooner can have enormous financial implications," says Pond. "It means greater Social Security income, longer time to let assets grow, and more time to save. I did a comparison of retiring at age 62 versus retiring at age 68, and by delaying that six years, it increased retirement income by over 80 percent."

Boomers also want work that they enjoy, work that is fulfilling, satisfying, and consistent with their values. As they become empty nesters, or reach a stage when they can focus on their own needs and desires, Boomers will look for work with a purpose as well as a paycheck.

Fifty-one-year-old Alexandra Bassil of Miami Beach, Florida, a public relations professional who is single, has a plan that will eventually allow her to do work that she loves with a schedule she controls. She is an expert in the art deco style of the old hotels and apartment buildings in Miami Beach, and plans to earn money giving architectural tours. She also earned a master's degree so she can teach part-time. "Someday I'd like to teach undergrads at a Florida college," says Alex. "I've also become a certified professional tour guide. I love South Beach and the art deco style here, and I want to be able to afford to work on something that I have a passion for as I age." Alex is a great example of a Boomer who is planning ahead, not to retire, but to work on her own terms.

Alexandra Bassil's Story

Alexandra Bassil had an early wake-up call. After years of making good money and living the high life as a single woman in San Francisco and New York City, Alexandra developed a chronic illness.

"I hadn't saved anything. Suddenly, I was out of work for a year and a half. I needed my family's help to recover. This was in my thirties, so I learned at a young age that you can't live without a safety net," says Alex.

Alex takes care of herself by working with a personal trainer, swimming almost every day, and getting holistic health treatments. She has recovered enough to work full-time but still needs what she calls "Cadillac health insurance" coverage.

"I realize that I'm living the life that I want right now. I own my own condo in Miami and I work from home for a New York-based company. I earned a master's degree last year and went to Paris with a friend to celebrate. But I've worked with a financial planner since 1992 to get where I am today."

Alex has been single her whole life and decided to work with Ellen Siegel, CFP, a financial planner in Miami who specializes in single people without children. Ellen helped Alex begin to save and save a lot! She puts aside 25 percent of her salary for retirement.

Because of her health scare and her single lifestyle, Alex has purchased catastrophic health coverage, long-term care insurance, and disability insurance. She's also spending more time working on her own well-being.

"I recently scaled back my work hours so that I could invest in myself and my health," says Alex. "I love my job because it's part of a life that I love. After the scare I had at age 36, I'm grateful to be doing so well physically and look forward to the next stage of my life. I won't really 'retire' in the traditional sense, I'll just be able to do what I love and have a more flexible schedule."

WILL YOU STILL NEED ME . . . WHEN I'M 65?

While millions of Boomers intend to keep working beyond 65, will employers need or want all the older workers who plan to stay in the game? Many businesses are still trying to shed veteran workers. Employees with high seniority generally have higher pay and more costly health benefits. Some employers also hold negative stereotypes of older workers, such as the following:

- They are not able or willing to keep up with new technology.
- They are too set in their ways to learn new skills or adapt to change.
- They are burned out or just marking time until they can retire.

In fact, many Boomers embrace computers and fully appreciate what they can accomplish with information technology. Boomers are often hardworking, committed, and dependable employees. They have strong work habits, emotional maturity, in-depth knowledge, and valuable life experience. Older workers are less likely to jump from one job to another, reducing employee turnover costs.

While employers are always looking to control costs, and cutting loose older workers is one way to do that, businesses will soon be facing a shortage of skilled labor. The U.S. has an increasingly knowledge-driven economy, requiring highly skilled workers. Companies expecting that a constant supply of skilled labor will always be available are not paying attention to demographics. Millions of Boomers are approaching retirement age, and the working age population behind them is much smaller. The Bureau of Labor Statistics reports that the U.S. workforce will grow by 12 percent in this decade, but that the growth rate will slow to 4 percent between 2010 and 2020, and to only 3 percent in the decade after that. That's an annual growth rate of just three-tenths of one percent starting in about 2020, when Boomers will range in age from 56 to 74. One way to minimize the impact of a slow-growing workforce is to keep older workers on the job longer.

Worker shortages are already showing up in many positions: nurses and health care aides, teachers, railroad workers, oil and gas engineers, plumbers and electricians, government managers, truck drivers, mechanical and aerospace engineers, accountants and financial analysts, and electrical utility workers. Even manufacturing workers are in short supply in some rural communities in the Midwest.

"Employers are going to see very slow growth in the labor force of young workers," says economist Alicia Munnell of Boston College. "They are just not going to see these hordes of college students coming out that they can fill their positions with. They have options. They can try to hire more women. They can try to hire more immigrants. They can try to do some outsourcing. They can use more technology. But in the end, I think they are going to have to recognize the need to more fully employ older workers."

Companies need to focus on retaining experienced workers rather than looking for ways to put them out to pasture. A business research group, The Conference Board, issued a 2006 report on older workers called "Age and Opportunity: Plan Strategically to Get the Most Out of a Maturing Workforce." The report concluded that "companies benefit by thinking of the issue of managing a maturing workforce as more than a negative (a problem to be dealt with). The companies that are succeeding in getting the most of older workers view the problem strategically as an opportunity for change within the organization."

The report recommends a three-part strategy: capture critical knowledge/expertise of retiring workers and transfer it; develop flexible work arrangements and benefits to retain valued retirement-eligible employees; and create a culture welcoming to employees of all generations. Some companies are getting the message.

A January 2007 report from CareerBuilder.com says, "One in five employers plans to rehire retirees from other companies or provide incentives for workers approaching retirement age to stay on with the company longer." Presumably, four in five have no such plans. Says economist Alicia Munnell: "I don't think most employers recognize yet that they are likely to face a worker shortage, and I don't think most employers are really in the process of changing their employment policies."

Career coach Jeff Williams in Chicago thinks it will take about a decade for most employers to realize that mature workers are an asset not a problem. "I don't think the older Boomers are going to benefit from this," he says. "Younger Boomers will see the turning point and be affected by the change."

Age Discrimination in the Workplace

Richard D. Glovsky is a nationally recognized trial lawyer and employment law attorney with the firm Prince, Lobel, Glovsky & Tye in Boston. He is a passionate advocate for civil rights, and he's also a Boomer. "There's absolutely no question that baby Boomers are victims of age discrimination, and in growing numbers," says Glovsky. He says that while age discrimination has always been with us, the sheer size of the baby Boom generation makes this a different time for both employees and employers.

"Older workers are almost always better paid workers," says Glovsky. "When a company gets into financial trouble, they often try to get rid of these people to help the bottom line."

Glovsky describes a typical case: "I recently represented a fifty-five-year-old male who worked for a public company. He was two years from retirement. He had stock options and other benefits that would have vested at retirement. He was one of the oldest and most highly regarded people at the company, but when they got into financial trouble, they let him go."

Glovsky's client sued, and the company settled before the case went to trial. However, Glovsky says that most employees are at a huge disadvantage when they try to pursue this type of case. "The cost of litigating age discrimination cases can be prohibitive and the big employers know that," says Glovsky. "They count on the fact that most people don't have pockets deep enough to pay to sue."

(continued)

Age Discrimination in the Workplace
(continued)

Glovsky says a lawsuit is not the only option for older workers. He advises Boomers to try to anticipate what might happen at work, and to study their employment manual to see if there is an in-house process to follow to resolve employment issues. "It's also important to stay on top of your own employment file," he says. "Filling a file with negative evaluations and reports is one way companies get ready to fire employees. It's important to debunk any negative reports with a positive response in a timely manner."

Age discrimination is not just about losing a job. It is also a factor when midlife workers are looking for work. Glovsky says this area is much trickier. It's hard to prove that you didn't get work because of your age. Glovsky advises Boomers who are seeking employment to know their rights. Employers cannot ask your age or ask any questions that might reveal your age, such as the date of your college graduation.

STRATEGIES FOR KEEPING BOOMER TALENT

Companies need to start by reexamining any misguided preconceptions about seasoned workers. Changing the mindset from viewing older workers as a burden to seeing them as individuals with skills, experience, and the potential to grow is a big first step. In time, companies will see that premature retirement is a waste of human capital they cannot afford.

To retain or attract Boomer employees, companies can adopt phased retirement plans and flexible schedules that allow workers to downshift as they approach the normal retirement age. These flexible arrangements may allow for part-time work, seasonal work, job sharing, telecommuting, callbacks for temporary assignments, and consulting contracts. Companies are already using many part-time and contract workers to keep down costs and increase flexibility. Now, they should design such programs for their own aging workforce.

Here is an example of how such an arrangement could work. An employee age 55 or older with at least five years of service could participate. The worker could scale back to a four-day week for a year or two, and then go to three days a week for a period of several years. The worker would keep full health coverage, but other benefits would be prorated based on hours worked. When possible, the worker could telecommute one or two days a week. The program could allow for a certain number of unpaid days off, at mutually agreed upon times. Such a program could stretch the employee's service several years beyond normal retirement, giving the company additional access to the worker's experience, specialized knowledge, contacts, and mentoring.

Boomers may opt for a phased retirement over several years, but they want to continue to make significant contributions, do high level work, and receive ongoing training to take on new challenges. They are seeking good health and retirement benefits, including counseling to help guide them through late-career transitions. Employers who do not adapt to the changing workforce may see some of their best talent leave and go to work for a competitor that offers more Boomer-friendly employment policies.

Some employers, like the Aerospace Corporation in El Segundo, California, allow for a trial retirement. If a worker decides to retire, they can test it out with a 90-day leave of absence. If they don't like it, they can come back to work.

The federal government also needs to take action to promote more flexible work arrangements. Pension laws make it difficult for employees to work for a company while receiving a pension from the company. Because of this, some people retire, start collecting a pension, and then go to work for a competing company. Furthermore, defined benefit pensions often base benefits on an employee's final three or five years of pay. Workers are discouraged from opting for a phased retirement, which reduces pay in the final years of work, and results in a less generous pension. These and other employment regulations need amending to encourage older workers to stay on the job.

STAYING IN THE GAME

Boomers should have no expectations of receiving a "velvet coffin" to close out their careers in leisurely fashion with great pay and benefits. Employers will only offer attractive retention programs if it is in their financial interest to do so. That means Boomers who continue working past normal retirement age will have to be sharp, focused, and productive. Late-career workers should keep up with changes in technology, learn new skills, and volunteer for new assignments. Global competition means change is constant. Responding to change is now a requirement for participating in the 21st century workforce.

If you plan to be working five years from now, whatever skills got you this far will not be enough to carry you the rest of the way. Lifelong learning is essential. Whether it is on-the-job training, taking courses online, or keeping up with trade journals, all workers need to continue adding to their bank of knowledge and skills. Many colleges report that middle-aged workers are signing up for more classes, and not "lifestyle" offerings, but substantive courses to enhance a current or future career.

Many experienced workers also enjoy mentoring younger colleagues. These relationships can be rewarding for both parties, and both can learn from each other. This is also an example of how flexible work programs can benefit companies, as veteran workers, who might otherwise be retired, remain on the job to pass along the subtleties of the business and the lessons of life.

Promises and Perils of Early Retirement

Jean Proulx Dibner raised four children first and had her career second. After 17 years as a homemaker, she decided to take some aptitude tests. They pointed her toward engineering.

"I went back to school when my children left home and studied computer science. I became an executive at Digital Equipment, developing projects for them," says Dibner. "I also worked at Apple and IBM doing much the same work."

In her fifties and near the end of her high-tech career, Dibner was a senior vice president of Avid Technologies, working 60 to 70 hours a week overseeing hundreds of employees and managing a budget of $50 million. When she saw the computer market beginning to slow down in the late 90's, she decided it was time "to do what I really wanted to do at that time in my life." She volunteered for an early retirement package.

"I no longer had children at home, I was newly divorced, so this was the time for me to figure out what I really wanted to do—and to get in touch with the dreams I had put aside as I'd been so focused on my corporate work."

The dream that Dibner wanted to pursue was her art. She had taken courses in sculpture at a museum school and wanted to have time to explore her creativity and develop her skills. She studied human anatomy, form, and technique. She spent long hours in her home studio, developing her own style. She found herself in transition, moving from her identity as "successful corporate executive" to "struggling artist."

"You work so hard to get yourself where you are, and a part of your identity is the title," Dibner says candidly. "Sometimes I'll be somewhere now, and somebody will say, 'What do you do?' and I'll say, 'I'm a sculptor.' They react like they think it's a hobby, not something meaningful and serious." But Dibner is serious. She has won national acclaim and prestigious awards, and her work has been shown in galleries across the country.

(continued)

Promises and Perils of Early Retirement *(continued)*

Today, she is able to sell her work for thousands of dollars. "I did have to put quite a bit of work into it. It's not like suddenly you're born a sculptor. I had to spend a lot of time doing pieces that I would give away before I got to the point where I was comfortable with actually selling my work."

Dibner says business skills and marketing savvy developed during her high-tech career came in handy as she developed her "retirement" career as an artist. But there were lurking financial concerns, worries that she had walked away from a high-paying tech management career. Dibner had stock in many of the companies she had worked for and counted on that as a safety net to help fund her retirement.

"I retired at the age of 58 with the thought I had really provided for myself financially. And then, with a big drop in the stock market, I realized I really wasn't OK," says Dibner. "I knew that I needed to have an income stream as well."

Dibner started teaching to supplement her other retirement income. And she continued to work hard developing her art and planning her new business. She says she had to keep fighting the fear of failure, and what she perceived as society's image of what she "should" be doing. She encourages others to do the same.

"I guess my advice would be not to accept the image that institutions have given you of what you're going to be at this stage in your life," says Dibner. "If we take charge, we really do have a lot of freedom in creating lives we want. You just have to be courageous enough, patient enough, and willing to work hard enough to fill in the gaps so that you can go where you want to go.

4

BLUEPRINT FOR A BOOMER CAREER CHANGE

Polling shows that about three-quarters of Boomers plan to continue working in retirement. That doesn't mean simply staying on the same old treadmill for an additional number of years. Having more free time, less stress, and flexible work schedules are all Boomer priorities. Most of us are interested in working part-time. Many say they want work that is satisfying, stimulating, and consistent with their values. In short, Boomers want it all in their "post-career" work lives. If we are going to keep working during "retirement," then it has to be meaningful work, and work on our terms.

For many, redefining retirement means a new career. Some people know just what they want to do. They have been toiling away at the job they have to do, while making plans for the work they want to do. Others know they want to make a change, but they are not sure which direction to follow. Deciding on a career change and making it happen is a big challenge. It takes a lot of soul-searching, planning, and determination. For some Boomers it's not a voluntary quest; they have to reinvent themselves because they have lost jobs in this unsettling era of downsizing, cost-cutting, and company mergers.

Transition coach Connie Adkins of Newton, Massachusetts, says Boomers entering this stage of life have to chart their own course. "It's really an extraordinary time in life. We are living longer; we are living healthier. There has never been a time of life like this before in the history of mankind. There are not the guideposts or the maps that we have for so many other times of life. We need each other or we need coaches to do this well. We are going to have many years ahead of us, almost as many as we've spent in our careers, so it's very important to do some planning."

TIME TO DREAM BIG

Many of us end up in careers more by accident than by design. A door opened up, we took it, and before we knew it, we were on our way with a family, a mortgage, and bills to pay. We set aside passions to meet our obligations. Some of us started out on the path we wanted, but the work was not as gratifying as expected, or we changed and our values and our careers came into conflict. Now is the time to revisit those early passions. It is time to rediscover yourself, and target your inner drive in a new direction.

"This is your time of life," says Jeri Sedlar, an expert on mature workforce issues and coauthor of *Don't Retire, Rewire!* Sedlar urges Boomers seeking a new path to list everything that excites them— their "drivers"—and to put them all into a big funnel. "Get everything imaginable into that funnel," says Jeri, "from your interests to your passions, discarded dreams, and incompletions. If you've ever found yourself saying, 'One of these days I'll . . . blank . . .' we want you to finish the sentence and get it into the funnel. You're sifting for gold, and that gold is going to lead you to a wonderful, rewired life."

"There are lots of ways to discover your passions," says transition coach Connie Adkins. "It's an internal process. It's really about paying attention to what you love, what engages you, what excites you and inspires you. You can find it in the books you read, the shows you watch, and the stories that engage you, and by paying a lot of attention to yourself. Keeping a journal is great. Talking to friends is another good way—people who similarly are looking to discover what's next for themselves."

This is no time to hold back. Do not allow self-imposed limitations and restrictions to thwart your thinking. Let your mind roam free. Entertain all possibilities and reconnect with any secret ambitions that have been bottled up for years. Now is the time to let them loose. This is about what you want to do, not what you have to do. You may not have considered that option for decades, and this is no time to let the opportunity slip away.

"We all feel the specter of loss and old age growing closer," says Connie Adkins. "And that gives a special urgency, and even a real preciousness to this time. It may be the last time to turn to those things and make them real."

Jim Fripp's Story

Boomers make career changes for many reasons. For fifty-seven-year-old Jim Fripp, it was a spiritual quest. Jim worked as a technician in local television in Boston for more than 30 years. He traveled the world doing audio production, and operated studio cameras for newscasts. The job paid well and included a good pension.

Jim's son, Sekou, was born with severe birth defects, suffering from quadriplegia, cerebral palsy, and cortical blindness. Sekou died at the age of 16, and Jim's life changed. "At his funeral, the casket ended up staying at the church overnight, and I stayed with it," Jim said. "And one of the voices that I heard, questions that I heard was, 'What are you going to do now?'"

Jim knew the answer. After many years of studying theology and counseling, Jim became a Baptist minister. He is helping his congregation raise money to build a new church that will include a health clinic to serve the community, "so that church is not just a Sunday thing; it's a seven-day-a-week thing," said Jim.

Jim gave up the security of his TV paycheck. He said he is going to trust the process and follow his new path. "I've always been involved with church and this is a road of fulfilling it, and having a more whole life, because you only have so much time. Just pay attention. Just walk that walk. God has been good so far to me."

LET THE JOURNEY BEGIN

Executing a successful career change is a process. Experts say it often takes more time and effort than people expect. It can be a frustrating and discouraging exercise, but for those who find the ideal career in midlife, it is a rewarding and uplifting discovery. It is best to start the process while still fully employed. That lets you keep your income and benefits while you explore your options. If you don't start searching until after you've quit your job, financial pressures may force you into a hasty decision. "A lot of Boomers are really kind of burned out when they retire, and they do want time to decompress, and that's understandable," says coach Connie Adkins. "But to begin to develop ideas for what you are going to do next when you retire or partially retire is very important. It's almost never too early to start pursuing your interests."

The three main stages to making a career change are the following:

- Self-exploration
- Research
- Action

It is a journey, and the process is similar to planning a complex trip. With an unlimited number of possibilities, you first have to decide where you want to go. What do you want to do and **explore**? Then you **research** your destination. How will you get there? Where will you stay? How much will it cost? Finally, it's time to hit the road and put your plans into **action**. Bon voyage!

SELF-EXPLORATION

Whether you use a stack of index cards or an imaginary funnel, the first step is to take inventory, to identify your dreams and your personal motivators. What gets you fired up? What makes you happy? What makes you proud?

Think back on your career to your most rewarding accomplishments. What was it about those peak experiences that clicked? Break it down into pieces. Was it the nature or purpose of the work? Was it the team interaction? Did you have a great boss who made everyone feel good? Analyze what you dislike about your current job. Understand what you want to leave behind, so you don't repeat the pattern as you move ahead.

Career expert Jeri Sedlar suggests looking at your appointment book. What kinds of events or meetings do you look forward to, and which ones do you dread? Keep noting the little clues about what feels right. Make a list of things that energize you. Consider such possibilities as the following:

- Hobbies
- Sports
- Hands-on activities like gardening, painting, or woodworking
- Volunteer work/helping others
- Mentoring or teaching
- Learning new things
- Favorite books, movies, television programs
- Conversations—what subjects get you engaged?
- Travel
- Food
- Favorite activities from childhood

Allow yourself to focus on what brings you satisfaction. Ask a spouse, family member, or close friend for suggestions. They have lived through your ups and downs and may provide valuable insights. Consider whether you need to make a complete career change or just a midcourse correction that eliminates the negatives of your current job, and keeps what you enjoy about work. You may find another position at the company you already work for, or a different job with another employer within the same industry. If you've been doing marketing work in the corporate sector, you may find similar work more satisfying at a nonprofit. The bigger the change you want to make—like to a totally different job in a very different line of work—the more challenging the search is likely to be.

Next, take inventory of your skills. Some experts recommend using index cards, one skill per card. Think broadly here. If you are a good writer or public speaker, take note. If you are also good at subtle skills like explaining complex matters or mediating disputes, get it down on a card. If you know how to use PowerPoint software, operate a power saw, or coach a hockey team in executing a power play, keep writing.

Are you good at organizing and managing? Do you have strong people skills? Give yourself credit. You may end up with a big pile of cards. Here again, guidance from those who know you best is a good reality check. You may end up adding a few cards to the pile, or you may discard a few if your loved ones are candid. (Maybe that chicken tetrazzini dish you make isn't as good as you think it is.)

Career coaches can help with your self-exploration. They can administer assessment tests, and help you to understand and act upon the results. Coaches can also keep you on track, lift your spirits in the hard times, and give professional guidance on opportunities that may arise. Coaches may also pose some deeper questions than you might ask yourself, such as the following:

- What would you do if you found you had only one year to live?
- What do you absolutely want to do before you get too old?
- Who do you want to be before it's too late?
- What would you do if you had $10 million?

Thinking hard and honestly about these questions will give you a better understanding of what really matters to you and what you should be looking for in the next phase of your life. It may help to write a personal mission statement that expresses who you are, what you would like to do, and where you'd like to go. Some career advisors recommend making a collage or visual representation of your favorite activities, passions, and areas of interest.

Make a list of what's important to you in a new job. Some of these items are practical:

- How much money do you need to make?
- Do you need full health insurance benefits in a new job?
- Do you need a 401(k) with matching contributions?
- How far are you willing to commute?
- Do you want flexible hours or the ability to telecommute?

Some of your needs may be more subtle:

- What kind of work culture do you want?
- Do an employer's values matter to you?
- Should your work have a strong social purpose?
- How important is it to do creative work?
- Do you like to work independently or have daily interaction with a team?

The International Coach Federation is a nonprofit organization formed by professionals who practice business and personal coaching. To learn more about the coaching process, and to locate coaches in your area, visit www.coachfederation.org.

RESEARCH

Having identified your skills and vital areas of interest and motivation, you can now begin to focus on new careers that are a good match. Select several appealing job categories and begin doing research. You can learn about new fields online, through books and magazines, by joining industry associations, attending conferences, and doing volunteer work.

One valuable online resource is the U.S. Department of Labor's *Occupational Outlook Handbook*. Published every two years, the handbook has extensive information on hundreds of different types of jobs. The *Occupational Outlook Handbook* tells you the following:

- Training and education needed
- Earnings
- Expected job prospects
- What workers do on the job
- Working conditions

Find the handbook on the Web at www.bls.gov/oco/home.htm.

While reading and surfing the Web are useful, the most valuable research comes from talking to people already in the field you are targeting. Finding those people means plugging in to your network. Boomers have been around a while, and many of us have hundreds of personal and professional contacts. Go through your Rolodex and make a list of people you can call for advice and guidance. If direct contacts don't have personal experience in the field you are researching, they may be able to refer you to someone who does. Spending a few minutes on the phone or grabbing a cup of coffee is not too much to ask, and many people will gladly help. If they decline, move on and don't take it personally. It won't be long before you find a friendly contact who will gladly share expertise about his or her occupation or industry.

If you are some years away from making a career change, remember to keep your network active and growing. Stay in touch with contacts. Spend time each week sending out a few emails or making some phone calls, just to check in. Attend industry meetings and follow up with people you meet. These connections will be very helpful, whether you make an orderly career change, or get jettisoned in a surprise corporate housecleaning. We are not suggesting this just to be opportunistic. Cultivating relationships is enjoyable and rewarding, and can make you more valuable in your current occupation. It is also a two-way street. Members of your network will contact you for assistance, and helping others is a gratifying experience. If you believe in karma, it won't hurt on that front either.

Many career changers assume they need to go back to school or obtain some additional formal training. That is sometimes true, but not always. School is costly and time consuming. Don't sign up for a degree program on the vague hope that it will somehow improve your chances. Make sure you really need to go that route to get to the promised land. Most Boomers are seasoned workplace veterans with a wide range of skills. You may have all the education you need to switch careers. Discovering the education requirements of your desired field is part of your research. But don't sell your existing set of skills short.

Some career moves clearly require more training. If you work in human resources and want to become a math teacher, fitness trainer, chef, yoga instructor, or financial planner, you will need to study and practice. This could involve several semesters of college course work, or a few months completing a certificate program. Get training in evening and weekend courses while still employed in your primary job. See if you can take courses through an education reimbursement plan, if your employer offers one. The more you can prepare for a career change while still getting a paycheck and benefits, the more quickly you can make your transition after leaving the mother ship. If you can make the change seamlessly, from the old job to the new one, that's terrific. But whether by chance or by choice, you may have to complete your search after leaving the old career behind.

ACTION

After soul searching and researching, it's time to get moving. Make lists of employers and contacts you want to meet with, and start making calls to set up appointments. Be prepared to emphasize why your skills are a good fit for a new employer. Anticipate any doubts a hiring manager may have about your experience or credentials, and have answers ready to address those issues.

Career experts say doing volunteer work related to the field you are targeting can be a great way to gain insights and to meet people in that sector. If you want to teach, volunteer to spend time around students in the appropriate age group. If you want to manage construction projects, help build a house with Habitat for Humanity. If you want to be a chef, volunteer in the kitchen of a local homeless shelter.

Working with a temporary employment agency may allow you to sample jobs in several related fields, and give you exposure to a variety of employers and hiring managers. Many people who work for temp agencies end up in full-time jobs at places where they did short-term assignments. Portland, Oregon-based VocationVacations lets you test-drive a new career by offering travel packages that include trying out your dream job. As the company's website says, "No need to quit your day job. No need to tell the boss. Just spend a couple days…working one-on-one with a VocationVacations mentor." This is not an inexpensive option, but it does provide a hands-on opportunity.

The career change search is not an easy process. "It can feel like spinning your wheels," says transition coach Connie Adkins. "We like to be certain. We like to be linear. We like to have one step spelled out after the next. But when you are searching, you can feel a little uneasy, uncomfortable, and even foolish at times."

Don't be discouraged. Despite unreturned phone calls, unanswered applications, fruitless Web searches, and even job interviews that don't close the deal, you will find a job. The harder you work at it, the sooner it will happen. Try to view looking for work as a job itself, and put in the hours that a job typically requires. Tell everyone you know what kind of work you are looking for. You never know if your bowling buddy's brother-in-law is looking for someone just like you. See if you can join a job search support group. It's a good way to get moral support and maybe a few ideas on searching for work. Whatever you do, keep making lists of things to do, and keep making concrete steps toward your goal.

Sandra Sessoms-Penny's Story

When Sandra Sessoms-Penny graduated from high school more than 30 years ago, a college education seemed like an impossible dream. As the daughter of migrant workers in Florida, she had few resources. But she joined the Air Force, and eventually used the GI Bill to get a master's degree in education. Now age 51, she's enjoying a new career and helping young people to build their futures.

Sandra spent 22 years in the Air Force. She started out as an aircraft electrician on a C-130 aircraft, and then became a paralegal and law office manager. As she approached retirement from the Air Force, she heard about a program called Troops to Teachers, which helps retiring military personnel make a transition into the field of education.

"I had been a Sunday school teacher in various places," says Sandra. "I had worked with kids and with my son and his friends, and I thought, 'Why not education?'"

Today Sandra is assistant principal at Windsor High School in Windsor, Virginia. She starts her day positioned right inside the school entrance. "I greet the students as they come into the building. Many of them may not have had a hello for the day," she says. "My job as assistant principal is to make sure it's a safe environment, a learning environment, and a fun environment for them."

Sandra is continuing her education and working toward a doctorate. "I do not have my doctorate yet," she says. "I'm one of the A-B-D students. 'All but the dissertation.' I do hope to go further with the doctorate degree. I hope to be eventually in a position to make policy. My next goal is to obtain a principalship."

Sandra has some advice for career-changing Boomers. "For someone who is in my age category, 50 plus, and you haven't really found your niche in life, I would recommend that you do volunteer work to find out what you really want to do, and start pursuing that. Realize that you have energy, energy, energy. And you don't know how well or how helpful you can be to someone by just reaching out—out of your comfort zone probably."

(continued)

Having made a successful career transition from the military to education, Sandra is excited about the future. "I feel great. I feel like I have a lot of energy. I have so much more to give. I am one of the blessed ones. I do still have my health, for the most part. I feel like my mind is still open to new ideas."

DON'T QUIT TOO SOON

While many Boomers dream of moving on to more meaningful work, some experts offer a warning: Don't quit your primary job too soon. Economist Alicia Munnell, director of the Center for Retirement Research at Boston College, says many Boomers have not saved enough to make an early exit from a good paying job with generous benefits. "The idea that you are going to stop your main job in your fifties and take on something that is fulfilling but doesn't pay very well doesn't seem realistic," says Munnell. "Most people are going to need to earn as much as they can throughout their fifties. There is going to be a time when you can shift to your dream job. But it's going to be in your early to mid-sixties, not your fifties."

Meaningful work with a less demanding schedule can mean lower pay and fewer benefits than a frontline corporate job. Giving up good pay and perks too soon can cost you later if you haven't saved enough. Taking full advantage of higher pay, matching 401(k) contributions, health coverage, education reimbursement, and other company benefits can help build a solid foundation for rewarding work in the post-career "retirement" years. Make sure the numbers add up before taking that jump to the next phase of your career.

For Boomers who see a career change occurring several years down the road, take advantage of your position to save aggressively for retirement. Those who build up a solid retirement savings account will have more options in a few years when they are looking to make a change. If your retirement savings are in good shape in your mid-fifties, you may be able to move on to more rewarding work sooner, and because you will not need to maximize your pay, you will have more flexibility in your work choices. But if your 401(k) balance is skimpy, you may have to keep on slaving away at a job you hate. Save conscientiously now to avoid a case of "golden handcuffs" later on.

5

TIME TO BE YOUR OWN BOSS?

The United States has more than 25 million businesses. Three-quarters of them have no employees other than the owner. At any given time, 1 in 10 American adults are in some stage of trying to start a new business. After three years, fewer than half those ventures will still be operating. Nevertheless, a 2003 AARP survey found that 15 percent of Boomers would like to start a business in retirement. Outplacement firm Challenger, Gray & Christmas reports that the number of workers age 55 and over who are self-employed increased by 28 percent between 2000 and 2006, the largest increase of any age group. Boomers are reaching for the brass ring of business owner-ship for many reasons. Burned out after long careers, they want to try something new. They want to be free of the corporate routines, the endless meetings, the bickering and backstabbing. Some have been laid off and discarded to the scrap heap of the global econ-omy, deemed permanently unemployable by corporations that want young hands willing to work long hours for short money. Starting a business may be risky, but so is sitting tight and biding your time in the "corpocracy."

The Boomer business model may range from a solo "lifestyle" business to a full-scale venture with rented space, employees, and plans for growth. Some people envision turning a hobby or personal interest into a part-time business to bring in some extra cash. Others, who have been toiling away in a corporate setting for years, plan to use their knowledge to exploit a specific market niche. Affluent Boomers are more likely to start a business than are their lower income counterparts. A 2004 RAND study for AARP on "Self-Employment and the 50+ Population" found that Boomers in the top income quartile are more than twice as likely to pursue self-employment than those in lower income brackets.

Becoming an entrepreneur has great allure. From Horatio Alger to Andrew Carnegie to Bill Gates, entrepreneurial heroes are woven through the American dream. After decades of working under the yoke of multiple bosses, some of them inept and uncaring, we yearn for the freedom to call our own shots. We want to bust out of our cubicles and hit the open road. It is a chance to do work that we care about, to make a living building something of value that can be passed on to our children. We want to be able to crank up Frank Sinatra singing "I Did It My Way" and say, "Yes, Frank. We certainly did!"

Not everyone is cut out to start and run a business, however. A big dream and lots of determination will help. But most entrepreneurs say that creating a successful business was much harder and took much more time than they expected. "If I had known how hard this was going to be, I'm not sure I would have tried it," is a common entrepreneurial refrain. Starting a business tests the knowledge, skills, and character of all who make the attempt. Fortunately, and despite formidable odds, hundreds of thousands of Americans do try it every year. And their grit, pluck, and commitment to succeeding are central to the vitality and dynamism of the U.S. economy.

CAN YOU CUT THE MUSTARD?

Entrepreneurs come in many shapes, sizes, colors, and personalities. But in sifting through the qualities that make a successful entrepreneur, certain traits stand out. Former high-tech CEO Peter Russo is director of the Entrepreneurial Management Institute at Boston University, where he teaches entrepreneurship. "When I think about whether someone should be an entrepreneur . . . generally one of the most important things is someone who is self-aware, someone who understands their own strengths and weaknesses, and is honest with themselves about those."

This means a frank appraisal about your entrepreneurial aptitude. Are you a self-starter? Are you good at working with others? Can you market and sell your product or service? Are you well organized and a good manager? Are you willing to put in the hours necessary to succeed? Can you handle ambiguity and deal with failure?

"Probably the second most important thing is someone with high self-esteem," says Russo. "You have to have a lot of confidence in yourself because there are going be times when it looks to the outside world that you have no chance, but a strong entrepreneur knows that they can do it, they can do things that other people may think of as impossible or very difficult. But if you don't believe in yourself, you are never going to take the chance to do that."

While we tend to mythologize about one or two guys in a garage creating the next big thing, no one does it alone. "One thing that I think every entrepreneur needs is a strong network," says Russo. "And you want to think about who do you know, who do you have contact with that can be helpful to you? Everyone uses a network when starting a company, and that could be people who can serve as suppliers, potential customers, advisors to your company, advisors to the whole start-up process. If you need to raise money, it's people who can help you do that, as well."

YOU AGAINST THE WORLD

Many Boomers have an entrepreneurial vision consisting of working at home in their sweatpants, walking the dog when they want to, and moseying down to the local coffee shop for an afternoon latte. The tools of the trade: telephone, computer, printer, Rolodex, FedEx. Not in the picture: depressing cubicle, grumpy bosses, and whining coworkers. Several trends are providing a favorable tailwind for this idyllic vision of work in the 21st century. High-speed Internet services, low-cost computing technology, and software products such as desktop publishing allow an individual to perform a sophisticated level of work that was unimaginable a decade ago. Corporate downsizing and outsourcing, the bane of many a Boomer, can be turned to our advantage as companies hire more outside contractors to perform specific services.

If you're a would-be solo artist, what do you need to do to get there? Should you start a service business? Become a consultant? Buy into a franchise? We consulted Jeff Williams, founder of BizStarters.com, who has trained and coached more than 4,000 new business owners. A fifty-plus business owner himself, Jeff specializes in showing his peers how to start a business that will be rewarding, inspiring, and manageable.

JEFF WILLIAMS INTERVIEW

Boomers: How do help your clients find a great business idea?
Jeff: I tell them to start by identifying the work they love to do most. Use your experience and do some research to look for an unsolved problem or unmet need related to your chosen work activity. You can make an attractive income solving the problem or meeting the need.

Boomers: How do I know if I can make a good living running my own business?

Jeff: Start by defining what you mean by a 'good living.' The finan-cial goal for many fifty-plus people is to supplement income they receive from their retirement savings. They don't need to earn a typical corporate salary. Once you set a dollar goal for your income, think about how many dollars you can earn in a typical transaction in your chosen business. Divide your dollar income goal by the dollars per transaction. Ask yourself, can I likely complete this number of transactions in a year, particularly if I run the business all by myself? It's not that difficult to create a business that generates $40,000 to $50,000 a year.

Boomers: How do I figure out how much money I need to invest to start my business?

Jeff: The big question here is, 'Do you want to turn your own idea into a business or purchase someone else's idea, either through buy-ing a franchise or an existing business?' A typical franchise purchase requires an investment of $70,000 or more during the first year. And buying an existing business can easily set you back $100,000 or more. On the other hand, you can often start a home-based business from scratch for less than $2,000 (add another $1,000 if you need to upgrade your computer).

Boomers: How do I make sure that my business fits my desired lifestyle?

Jeff: The vast majority of Boomers say they want to continue to work. But, they also emphasize that they want to work in a way that provides a more satisfying balance between their work lives and leisure time. To help assure that you find this a better fit, start by writing down a specific description of the lifestyle features you desire such as hours of work per week, type of people you want to work with, how much time you want to take off each year, etc. Use these specific lifestyle features to assess each business idea you're considering. If you don't realistically think that any given idea matches your lifestyle criteria, go on to the next concept.

Boomers: What are the different methods I can use to turn my idea into a business?

Jeff: There are 10 popular categories, or business models, for small business today. They are the following:

1. create and sell an information product
2. provide advice as a consultant
3. convert a hobby into a business
4. invent and market a new product
5. run a retail store
6. run a webstore
7. distribute products or supplies
8. run a restaurant
9. sell personal or home services
10. sell business services

Boomers: What are the key ingredients for entrepreneurial success?

Jeff: All kinds of people start businesses. But all successful business owners share a set of common traits:

- They start with a business concept that clearly solves a problem or satisfies a need for a particular group of people.
- They have a clear understanding of their business expenses.
- They are disciplined in operating the business.
- They continually experiment with imaginative marketing activities.
- They carefully manage their money and protect their profit.
- They have a team of talented advisors and service providers to support their work.

Jeff Williams offers dozens of free articles on his website at www.bizstarters.com.

FROM HOBBY TO BUSINESS

The idea of turning a hobby into a moneymaking operation is a tantalizing prospect. After all, a hobby is what you do for fun. Who doesn't want to have fun while turning a profit? That's just what happened to Susan and Peter Milsky. After working as office manager for her husband's dental practice, Susan retired and began thinking about what to do next. "I was looking for some new direction, a hobby, something to fill my time," she says. "And I saw that they were giving a class in glass jewelry at a local arts center, and I said, 'I think I will try this,' not intending for it to be anything other than a hobby. I just loved it so much that I asked the teacher if he could order me a kiln so I could continue working at home."

Meanwhile, Peter Milsky was planning to retire after 34 years in dentistry. "I didn't really have any plans as to what I wanted to do. I have a lot of other interests. I love to fish and play tennis and golf and do things like that, but that wasn't going to be enough. So when Susan got involved with this jewelry, she said, 'Well you're a dentist, you can probably drill holes in things,' so I said, 'Yeah, I probably can,' and I started wire wrapping some of the jewelry with stainless steel fishing wire. Plus, I had the basic skills from being a dentist. I knew how to work with my hands. I had worked with wire; I had done a lot of orthodontics as a dentist, and it just sort of fell into place."

They started taking their creations around to trade shows and galleries. Wearing some of their unique pieces, Susan won many compliments from gallery owners, and more important, a growing book of orders. A new business was born almost by accident. "A lot of the fun is learning how to start something new from scratch, to take this little thing and build it into a business," says Peter. "The two of us are constantly talking about it: how to work it out, how to make our displays better, how to market things better."

They also marketed themselves to a cruise ship line, getting a Caribbean cruise in return for giving jewelry lessons as an educational activity for passengers. In starting their business, they created an entirely new chapter for themselves. They had already worked together in the dental office; now they have taken their partnership in a totally unexpected direction. "I am following my passion and doing what I want to do," says Susan. "I wake up and it's like, 'What do I want to work on today?' I am so thrilled to have found this."

For Peter, it's been a huge midlife change in his self-image and his personal style. From buttoned-down medical professional to creative artist, he has found a satisfying niche that draws upon his old skills but opens up entirely new vistas. "I enjoy it. I dress differently now than before, and I'm wearing jewelry that I didn't wear before. And it's just like a new life."

RISKY BUSINESS

Taking the plunge means taking a risk. When you start a business, you devote time, energy, and financial resources. You also sacrifice the opportunity to make money pursuing a safer, if less satisfying, alternative. If the enterprise fails, you lose on all counts, although you come away with some valuable life lessons. For those starting their first business, taking a few precautions can increase the likelihood of success.

"The worst pitfall I would be concerned about if I were starting a company today would be that I don't have all the resources I need to be successful," says Boston University's Peter Russo. "The most common example of that is somebody who doesn't have enough money to fund the start-up of his company, and they start the company anyway. They hope things will go right, and things typically don't. Everything tends to take longer and cost more money than you expect it to. And so if you don't have the money to do what you think you are going to do, and a cushion on top of that, you are going to run out of money. The worst time to be looking for additional money is when you've spent all the money you had, and not achieved the goals you had set for yourself."

Experts warn, however, that Boomers should not put their retirement savings on the line to start a new business. Most Boomers have not saved enough money for retirement anyway, but to risk a nest egg that may have to last 30 years or more on a new business venture is foolhardy. It just compounds the risk of what is already a risky endeavor. For Boomers under age 59 and a half, breaking into retirement savings also incurs a 10 percent penalty to the IRS, in addition to the taxes due from cashing out of a retirement plan.

Business start-up advisors recommend that entrepreneurs use other funding sources including modest amounts of non-retirement personal savings, home equity loans, Small Business Administration loans, and funding from partners, family, friends, and angel investors (wealthy individuals who enjoy backing small-scale enterprises that they find interesting). Keeping business costs down is critical in the start-up phase. Some "lifestyle" businesses can be launched for just a few thousand dollars.

If your business is going to have one or more partners, choosing the best people to work with is critical. The wrong choice could doom your venture from day one. Peter Russo lists this challenge right below adequate financing: "Perhaps a second biggest pitfall that I've seen entrepreneurs follow is that rather than taking the best person you can find to join your team, you take friends or relatives who are close by because you have known them all your life, and you assume that you'll have a great time together. The best advice I can offer is to hire the best people you can find. Don't assume that just because you have a good personal relationship with somebody that they are necessarily the best fit for your company."

FROM PASSION TO PAYCHECK

Jane Carolan is an architectural historian. She has worked for several architectural firms, and has been a preservation consultant on a number of major construction and building rehabilitation projects. But she was looking for more autonomy and flexibility in her work. She took a winter off to ponder the future. "I realized more and more that, yeah, I'm going to be retiring," said Jane. "And I don't want to just drift into it. It's your last opportunity, really, to give back, to take in, and to have a creative life."

Looking for guidance on starting a business, Jane consulted a career coach who helped her to develop a service she could provide doing work that she loved. They came up with House Tales, a business aimed at affluent owners of historic homes in New England. Jane prepares a house history, which contains a description and analysis of a home's architectural style. She does extensive research using deeds and probate records, genealogical histories, family papers, maps, and historic photographs to compile a comprehensive dossier on the properties.

"I love to do research and write," says Jane. "I would do it no matter what. I would be doing my own projects. But to keep doing this just feels like the perfect fit, and it's something that will keep me young. So, I'm excited. I think it's a perfect segue way."

Jane needs to keep generating income and saving for the future. "One of the first things I said to my coach is that I feel like I have about 10 good years of work in me, and I'd like to take that energy for 10 years and the money that I'm going to make, and just gear all that to retirement."

Jane succeeded at taking work she loved doing and creating her own space in the economy. It may not carry the pay and perks of a corporate job, but it's providing other, more important rewards. "At this point in my life, in my fifties, I feel really focused and really confident, and really feel like I am going to take off in a way that I never have before."

MAKE A BUSINESS PLAN

A good business starts with a good plan. A written plan forces you to sit down, think about the business, and organize your ideas. The plan consists of a clear description of the business concept, specifics on how to implement the idea, and a realistic assessment of how to make a profit. The plan should address such key areas as the following:

Description of the Business
Who owns the company?

What type of business is it? Sole proprietor, Corporation, S Corp, etc.?

What is the product or service?

What is the name of business?

Who are the target customers, and why will they buy the product?

What is the competition?

How will the product or service be made and distributed?

Where are the business location and facilities?

Marketing
How will customers find out about the product or service?

What promotion and advertising will be most effective?

Who will carry out marketing plans?

Finances
How much will it cost to start and operate the business?

What is the source of start-up capital?

What equipment will need to be purchased or leased?

What will it cost to produce the product or service?

How should the product be priced?

What are the projected sales?

Management
Who makes key decisions?

Who performs various functions?

Who will handle the books and make sure all taxes are paid on time?

Who are the suppliers?

Who are the advisors to the business?

What insurance is needed?

What licenses or permits are required?

While not an exhaustive list, this illustrates many of the key areas to consider before launching your enterprise. Just diving in and assuming you can improvise your way through all your challenges is a recipe for trouble. The more you plan in advance, the better prepared you will be, and the more likely you are to succeed.

The Small Business Administration (SBA) of the federal government has valuable advice for entrepreneurs on its website www.sba. gov). The SBA also guarantees loans to qualifying small businesses, and can connect entrepreneurs with advisory services such as SCORE, which counsels small business owners. The SBA also has a quick summary of advice for business start-ups:

- Look for new ideas.
- Keep it simple.
- Start small.
- Try, try, try again.

BUSINESS BASED ON VALUES

A Boomer in her late forties, Robin Chase, cofounded a car rental company called Zipcar in 1999. "We wanted to make getting a car as easy and convenient as getting cash from an ATM," says Robin. "In order to accomplish that, we had to use the Internet and wireless data transmission in a way that was really a seamless user experience."

Zipcar is for city dwellers who don't want to own a car, but who occasionally need access to a vehicle. Zipcars are parked at strategic locations in about a dozen U.S. cities and in London, England. Robin explains how it works: "Members can make a car reservation either online or by telephone, and it takes about 30 seconds. That reservation gets sent wirelessly to the car, and the car will only open to the right person at the right time."

Members can rent a vehicle for a few hours or a few days at a time, returning the car to its parking spot, and paying automatically by credit card. Zipcar covers the cost of maintenance, insurance, and gasoline. The service saves urban residents the burdensome cost of buying, insuring, maintaining, and parking a car in congested urban areas. Zipcar says its service has induced thousands of people to give up owning a car, resulting in less pollution and traffic congestion.

"The wonderful thing about being an entrepreneur," says Robin, "is that I feel like the conductor of a symphony, and that you are pulling together all these different people to create your vision. It's thrilling that you can look back and say all these people worked together and produced this wonderful and beautiful thing." But it was not easy. With major capital expenditures, complicated technology, and licensing deals in multiple cities, Zipcar was a complex business to launch. Success was not always a sure thing. Married and the mother of three, Chase says, "I couldn't have done it without my family. There were days when I came home ready to completely give it up. And my family was there to say, 'You're great and we love you no matter what is going on.'"

For entrepreneur Robin Chase, the business stemmed from her deeply held values. A resident of Cambridge, Massachusetts, Robin is a champion of an urban lifestyle where people can walk to shops and services, use mass transit, and occasionally rent a Zipcar. The business was also built around Robin's passion to create an online community of urbanites committed to reducing their use of fossil fuel. "I have a strong desire to leave the world a better place. I feel like we are entering into a difficult time ahead with global warming and fossil fuel being depleted. And I want my children to have a wonderful quality of life, and I want the world's children to have a wonderful quality of life."

Robin left the CEO position at Zipcar a few years ago, and has started another company, Meadow Networks. It is a consulting firm focused on using technology to improve urban transportation. She looks forward to a long and productive future. "When I was about 25, I worked at a company that was started by a woman when she was 75, and she was still running it in her nineties. I looked at that woman and I thought, 'I want to be like that. I want to start something when I'm 75 and think that I've got another 25 years in me.'"

Part Three

HOME

6

THE NEXT BOOMER HOUSING BOOM

Get any group of Boomers together, and sooner or later, the conversation drifts around to real estate. What is happening to home values? Did you hear about the Smiths putting their house on the market? Should we sell our home in the suburbs and move into town, or just sit tight? Can you picture yourself in a high-rise condo in Florida? People like to dream, share stories, and weigh their options. Our feelings about real estate are a complex brew of financial issues, emotional ties, practical considerations, and flights of fancy. Real estate and the Boomer experience have been intertwined since the very beginning.

The post–World War II baby boom has driven housing trends for more than half a century. When the GIs—our parents—came home, they started families and had a record number of children. They got low interest loans from the government and bought homes in newly created suburbs. In the late '60s and early '70s, as the oldest Boomers got out of school, they needed rental units and apartment construction surged. When Boomers married they bought starter homes, and later on, traded up to larger suburban houses, all of which fueled more home building. By the '90s, Boomers were opting for luxury and the McMansion craze was in full swing. Now, as Boomers approach retirement, their future housing preferences are the subject of much speculation, innumerable polls and studies, and big investments by developers eager to cash in on emerging trends.

Where and how Boomers decide to live will be determined by many factors including their finances, work plans, family considerations, health status, weather, and lifestyle preferences. Some will head for the simple pleasures of small town life, others will opt for a fast-paced urban experience. Many plan to stay in their current home, others will pack up and move to a foreign country. Boomers have a wide array of alternatives, and what they select at age 60 or 65 may not be the final chapter. With decades still to live, many of today's Boomers will reside in a variety of settings as their lives and needs evolve.

"Each of these things—like moving to retirement communities, moving back into urban condos, retrofitting homes—are happening," says Wellesley College economist Karl "Chip" Case, one the nation's leading authorities on housing. "And since there are so many baby Boomers, they are all trends that matter. Which ones will turn out to be the dominant ones, it's just impossible to say. They are all true, and they're all happening at the same time."

Whatever housing decisions Boomers make, it will be a big story, just because of our sheer numbers. If 10 percent of our generation decide to move into active adult communities, that's nearly eight million people, and more than four million units of housing. If 1 Boomer in 20 joins a cohousing development, it will revolutionize an emerging form of communal living. We are housing trendsetters and will continue to be for years to come.

BOOMER BELLWETHERS

A 2006 study conducted for Hanley Wood, a publishing and trade show company for the housing and construction industries, looked at future housing preferences for affluent "leading edge" Boomers. Those are home owners ages 50 to 60 with household incomes of at least $100,000, dubbed "Boomfluentials" in the study, and seen as a bellwether of emerging trends.

According to the survey, these are the housing plans of those upscale Boomers who are closest to retirement:

Buy a different or new home	35%
Stay in current home as it is	21%
Design or build new home	17%
Stay in current home, but remodel	15%
Buy a second home	12%
Rent apartment or home	1%

Source: DYG, Inc.

Note: Percentages may total 100 due to rounding of numbers.

Nearly half of those surveyed plan to keep their existing home, including those doing renovations and those buying a second home. Slightly over half intend to move, with one in six "Boomfluentials" planning to build a new home. Other key findings are the following:

- 58 percent prefer a smaller home in the future.
- 72 percent want to live in a single-family detached home, down from 89 percent who do so now.
- 67 percent want to live in the suburbs, a slight decline from the 73 percent who currently reside in the 'burbs.
- 14 percent would like to live in a rural setting, up from the current 8 percent.
- 16 percent want to live in an urban environment, down from 18 percent who are currently city residents.

The big winner in the Boomer migration may well be rural communities, with both suburban and city locales losing population. Those surveyed showed a preference for moving to states in the South Atlantic region and the Mountain states. The Middle Atlantic area and the Northeast are likely to see a Boomer exodus.

While nearly 6 in 10 want a smaller home, the survey showed Boomers want to "downsize," not go "downscale." That points to a growing demand for high quality smaller homes. A 17-point drop in preference for a single-family detached home indicates growing demand for upscale condos, with no grass to cut or driveways to shovel. "Boomfluentials" also showed strong interest in moving to a region with a lower cost of living, better climate, and to homes where they can live comfortably on one floor.

WHAT'S YOUR PLEASURE?

Because we are all unique individuals with our own stories, our own issues, and our own plans and dreams, decisions about where to live are highly personal. Do we want to stay close to grandchildren? Does an aging parent need us to live nearby? Do we have great friends that we can't imagine leaving? Is it getting harder to face another long winter? Can we afford to handle the upkeep of the big family home? So many vital issues are all wrapped up in one big decision.

Pulte Homes, the nation's largest developer of active adult communities, conducts frequent surveys of baby Boomers and their housing preferences. Their 2005 survey showed that of younger Boomers (ages 41 to 49 as of 2005), 59 percent plan to move to a new home in retirement. Among older Boomers (ages 50 to 59), 50 percent indicate a desire to buy a new home for retirement.

Of those willing to move, 66 percent of older Boomers want to move for a better community lifestyle, and 54 percent would seek a warmer climate. Just under half (47 percent) of all poll respondents (ages 41 to 69) say staying within three hours of family would be an important consideration about where to relocate in retirement.

Our personal family role models were fairly typical. Our parents kept their homes in the Northeast after retirement but became Florida "snowbirds" as soon as the holidays were over. Some of their friends settled in Arizona. The attraction was warm weather, a life full of leisure time, golf almost every day, beachcombing or gardening, and dinner with friends.

While older Americans still migrate to Florida, that flight pattern may change with the Boomers. Many of our friends say that's their parents' retirement; it will be different for us. There seems to be a real estate "generation gap" here. Hiding out in a beautifully manicured gated community with people of similar age and socioeconomic backgrounds does not have wide appeal for the Boomers. Our generation is considering a variety of lifestyles that fit the goal of remaining actively engaged in the real world. These include moving to the city, living near a college campus, cohousing and group living, family compounds, and relocating to a foreign land.

With all the variations on the housing theme, we see most Boomers opting for one of five broad choices, each with its own pluses and minuses:

> **Age in place:** Keep the old homestead; renovate to fit empty nester lifestyle.
>
> **Age in community:** Cash out of the big house, and downsize to nearby smaller home or condo.
>
> **Age in region:** Take profits from urban or suburban home, and move one to two hours away.
>
> **Relocate:** Move far away for a financial windfall and/or a new lifestyle.
>
> **Combo plate:** Keep the old house, or downsize within the community, and buy (or continue using) a second home for seasonal getaways.

Within these categories are various subthemes, which we will explore in the next chapter. But first, we analyze the pros and cons of these five major options.

AGE IN PLACE

As Dorothy told Auntie Em in *The Wizard of Oz,* "There's no place like home." It's where the kids grew up. It's where we know the neighbors, have friends, and go to church. It's as comfortable as settling onto a stool at *Cheers* bar, even if not quite *everyone* in town knows your name. Aging in place has strong appeal to many Boomers. If any of the kids need to come home, there's plenty of room. (Well, maybe not plenty, but there's room in a pinch.)

If extended family has remained nearby, those connections are meaningful as we age. If you need to continue working, this is where you have the contacts, know the territory—better than moving to Tucson and starting a consulting practice from scratch. Your doctor, dentist, lawyer, and accountant remain nearby. And don't forget the trustworthy electrician, plumber, and car mechanic who have served in good stead for years.

If you can afford to "age in place," it's a great option. But it can carry a big price tag. Staying in the house which served admirably while raising children can be a luxury in late middle age. The home may be too large for a couple or single who has only occasional visits from family members. The taxes, maintenance, and heating bill are all regular reminders that keeping the "big house" going may be an expensive exercise in clinging to the past.

Staying in your residential "comfort zone" can also mean that considerable equity is tied up in the property. Your house may have greatly appreciated over the years, and your mortgage may be just about ready to burn. But all you can do with that equity is live inside of it, or borrow against it. Selling the property and freeing up its value could allow you to do more travel and enjoy a fuller lifestyle. You could move to a less expensive home and invest the profits to provide a stream of income. There is obviously much more to consider in home ownership than a hard-boiled financial calculation, but if money is tight, you might not want to be house-rich and fun-starved.

MAKING THE CASE FOR HOME COOKIN'

A financial planner we know seems to personify positive attitudes about aging in place. Dee Lee, CFP, and author of *The Complete Idiot's Guide to Retiring Early*, has lived for many years in a small, rural community northwest of Boston. It's the community where she and her husband raised a family, and are now empty nesters. Dee knows that life in the Northeast will continue to be expensive. She prefers to plan for that expense, however, rather than think about moving to a cheaper part of the country.

We were talking with her about someone who had moved from the metropolitan New York City area to Kansas, and had saved a bundle in housing and living expenses. "It sounds like a great idea," said Dee. "Take the equity out of the house, move to someplace exotic, or where I can afford everything, but the reality is that some of the things that you had on the East and West Coast may not be available in Kansas. Plus your friends may not be in Kansas, and definitely your family's not there. If you've got grandbabies you may want to be at least a car ride away."

Dee is an active member of her community and her church. Leaving all those relationships and activities behind to "cut the overhead" is too big a price to pay. "I prefer staying in the same place because there's a comfort level being able to walk into the post office and say good morning and have everyone yell, 'Good Morning, Dee!' There's a comfort level going to the church I've gone to for 38 years, of being part of the Christmas pageant as I've been doing for many, many years. I like that feeling of comfort that it brings. But it's also my support system."

A well-known public speaker and radio commentator, Dee has particular expertise on issues of women and money. "The scary thing is, as a woman, I need to plan for 30 years, and I need to plan probably to be alone, because women outlive men on average by 7 years." All those hometown connections may someday be of great assistance. "If you live in a small community where everybody knows your business, people think that's bad. But it's not! In times of crisis it's good, because people are there to help, people are there to do things for you.

"Housing is going to be one of your major expenses and you need to plan for it," says Dee. "People say, 'Well, I'll live in a condo.' That's great, but what about the condo fees, what about the taxes, inflation? We cannot run away from it, and we need to plan, especially in retirement. The things we want—housing, services, medical care—are all expensive." For Dee, it's better to face all that in a community where she has supports rather than as a lonely refugee in Sunshine City Retirement Village.

Put It in Reverse to Move Forward

One way to "age in place" but still gain access to a home's equity is through a reverse mortgage. It's called a reverse mortgage because instead of paying the bank, the bank pays you.

A reverse mortgage enables home owners age 62 and up to convert part of the equity in their home into tax-free income without having to sell the home, give up the title, or take on a new monthly mortgage payment.

"A reverse mortgage lets you tap into the equity you have in your house," says former *New York Times* financial columnist Fred Brock. "You can take the money as a lump sum, or a stream of income, or even a reserve account you can write checks against as you need it. So, there are lots of ways you can take a reverse mortgage, and stay put if your income goes down in retirement."

According to the National Reverse Mortgage Lenders Association, the most popular option—chosen by more than 60 percent of borrowers—is the line of credit, which allows you to draw on the loan at any time. The industry is expecting explosive growth once the first Boomers hit age 62 in 2008. The amount that can be borrowed is determined by a variety of factors including the borrower's age, property value, and prevailing interest rates. In general, the older you are and the more valuable your home, the more money you can get.

(continued)

Put It in Reverse to Move Forward
(continued)

When the house is sold, or the owners die, the lender receives its money back plus interest. The amount due the lender can never exceed the value of the home. If the home sells for more than is owed to the lender, the seller or their estate receive the balance.

To qualify for a reverse mortgage, the primary mortgage on the property must be paid off in advance or paid off using funds from the reverse mortgage. These mortgages have fees that can be substantial but can be paid with funds from the loan. A reverse mortgage diminishes, and can totally eliminate, a homeowner's equity in their property. Your heirs may not love it, but a reverse mortgage provides a flexible tool for paying off debts, making home repairs, travel, or giving your lifestyle a boost without having to move. The AARP website has an excellent report with more details on how reverse mortgages work. Go to www.aarp.org/money/revmort.

AGE IN COMMUNITY

Housing equity for Americans over age 50 was estimated to be $2.5 trillion in 2000, and has grown even larger in recent years according to the 2006 study "Housing Trends Among Baby Boomers," conducted for the Research Institute for Housing America. The report called that equity "the most important non-pension asset in household portfolios, and a large reserve of untapped wealth." Aging in community is a way to tap into that wealth. This is the classic "have your cake and eat it too" scenario, where you sell your house for a profit, but stay close to home to enjoy many of the benefits of "aging in place." This usually means downsizing to reflect the need for less living space. The new home may be a smaller house, condo, or apartment within a half-hour drive of the old homestead. The principal benefit is financial. By selling a large "family" house and moving into something smaller, it is possible to make enough profit to either buy the next home outright, or to have a much smaller mortgage. The cost and effort to maintain the new residence should be reduced. Property taxes, heating bills, and insurance also go down.

Tax laws are generous in supporting this strategy. Couples selling a principal residence can earn a tax-free capital gain of up to $500,000 on their federal taxes. Single taxpayers can pocket $250,000. Sellers qualify for the tax break if they have owned the home and it has been their main residence for at least two of the past five years. For Boomers on a budget, selling a home is a great way to free up cash for living expenses, travel, or starting a business. It's also a better use of the community's housing stock if another growing family can occupy a large home, while empty nesters live in space that suits their needs.

While this strategy may involve moving to a different part of town or even to a nearby community, the benefits of being close to family, friends, church, doctors, professional contacts, and familiar haunts remain intact. While retaining local roots, such a move can also be exciting. A new community means new experiences, new neighbors, different restaurants and shops, and a change in commuting (maybe the new location will reduce dependency on the automobile).

SIMPLIFY

Downsizing is an opportunity to simplify, remove the clutter, reduce energy consumption, and focus on what's important. Those of us who have raised a family in one home for many years have accumulated tons of stuff. When the kids leave home, they leave stuff behind. The household's rarely used belongings are packed away in the attic, basement, closets, back porch, and garage. Moving out of the "big house" is a great opportunity to eliminate all that extra baggage. Some of it can be sold in a tag sale or on eBay. Much of it can be tossed. Children should be given a "last call" opportunity to collect what they want before it heads to the dumpster. (Many a Boomer, including Mark, lost his baseball cards in just this sort of housecleaning.)

We have personally experienced two of these big cleanups, one for Nancy's parents' house, and one of our own. Before moving, we found a dealer who brought a dumpster to the house and helped us to sort out our stash. He carted off the junk and we sold the useful items. But we also discovered how emotionally attached we can be to our possessions. What do you do with your twenty-five-year-old daughter's old stuffed animals and second grade penmanship papers? It is difficult to part with some items, and that's fine. But most of it can go, and it feels good to clear out the trash and start fresh.

GET OUT THE CALCULATOR

Despite the benefits of aging in community, the flip side is that making a move within the same geographic area may yield a disappointing profit when all the dealing is done. Smaller homes and condos may also be expensive in what is, essentially, the same real estate market.

Selling a $500,000 home can mean a broker commission of $25,000 to $30,000. The move will cost a few thousand more. Some "downsizers" end up renting storage units, adding a new monthly charge. Use a sharp pencil to carefully determine the financial implications of making a move. If you end up with nearly the same monthly expenses, little extra money in the bank, *and* a smaller house, it's not exactly a move made in heaven.

Another consideration is that once you leave the "big house," it is much more difficult to help an adult child who needs to come home for a while—"a boomerang kid." With college loans, credit card debt, and stingy starting salaries in many occupations, some young adults need the refuge of their parents' home while they get their lives on track. Providing that option is much more challenging if you have scaled down from a 2,500 square foot, four-bedroom house to a 1,200 square foot, two-bedroom condo with one and a half baths. Nevertheless, it is not worth it for Boomer parents to lose money by hanging on to the homestead merely for the possibility that a child may need support. It would be better to cash in by making a move, and then provide financial support to a child, if possible. Another option is to buy a new home with one more room than you need. This can serve as an office or exercise room, but also be available for a boomerang kid or other visitors. See the story of a couple with two boomerang kids in Chapter 14.

Single and Downsizing

Alison Goulder is a special education teacher who lived and worked for many years in an upscale suburb of Boston, before moving to a condo in a nearby community. She is divorced and has two adult children, one son in college and a daughter who has graduated and is on her own. We spoke with Alison about her decision to change her lifestyle and save for retirement in her fifties.

Boomers: How did becoming an empty nester affect your thinking and planning?

Alison: I had been looking to downsize for a couple of years knowing that my kids were going to be off and I felt that I didn't need to be in the community that I was in any longer for the schools. Upkeep of my house was becoming really challenging. I'd been on my own for about 10 years and the cost of maintaining it was actually pretty exorbitant.

Boomers: How did you decide where you would live once you sold the family home?

Alison: I wanted to move into a community that welcomed single, older adults. I had a friend who was a Realtor and she basically helped me figure out what properties would be good to look at. I wanted a place where I could welcome my two children home and they would always have a place to stay. I found a condo that fits my life now. I know people in the community. It felt like the right place when I saw it. The new place is a town house, and it's vertical, so it's going to keep me young and spry climbing up three flights of stairs every day!

(continued)

Single and Downsizing *(continued)*

The neighborhood is more urban. I can walk out the door, cross the street, and be at the post office. I can cross the street in the other direction and be at the library. I go in another direction and I can be on the bike path. But I can also walk a bit and be near houses that resemble my old neighborhood. So it's not this total rift of moving from suburbia to downtown Boston. I wasn't quite ready to make that shift.

Boomers: How did the move change your financial picture?

Alison: I had good timing. I knew that there were going to be a lot of houses on the market very, very shortly. I decided if I could sell and find a new place, I would be in a better financial situation. What I bought will be more rentable in the future when I retire. And if I decide to travel or work abroad, this will be an easier place for me to rent than a freestanding house in a suburban community.

I'm not making a huge profit on the house that I sold, but the good news for me is that the cost of upkeep of the new place will be considerably less than the house. So in that sense, I think I'm coming out ahead.

Boomers: Have you always been careful about financial planning and budgeting?

Alison: I didn't know a whole lot about finances until both my parents passed on and the finances just landed in my lap! I had to have a quick education. I didn't really plan until very recently. Now I'm forced to really take a closer look at what I can and cannot afford.

It's a different experience for me to live on a budget. I've never had to think about it in those terms and now I actually do. I'm also trying to teach my children that they have to live on a budget. It's quite a challenge when they have never had to!

There are certain things I can afford and certain things I can't. But at this time in my life, I know what things are important and what I don't really need.

AGE IN REGION

This is a more ambitious move that will be popular with Boomers who have tight retirement budgets, but don't want to move too far from the old neighborhood. It involves selling the urban or suburban home and moving an hour or two away to a more affordable area. This is a way to capture the big run-up in real estate prices that has occurred in many areas, while staying within a reasonable driving distance of hometown connections.

Economist Karl Case of Wellesley College says home equity can help to boost the Boomer standard of living. "The equity in your house also pays for a house out of state that would be much less expensive. So one of the options that Boomers have, if they live in these high-price areas, is . . . to leave and improve their standard of living. And a fair number of them are exercising that option."

One hypothetical example of such a move is from the New York City area to Bethlehem Township, Pennsylvania, just under two hours from midtown Manhattan. We looked up two properties for sale on the same day in February 2007. In the New York suburb of Larchmont, a three-bedroom, two-and-a-half-bath property was listed at $729,000. Judging from the photo it was not a trophy home, but Larchmont is an affluent town, so prices are high. In Bethlehem Township, a four-bedroom, two-and-a-half-bath colonial with a two-car attached garage was listed for $315,000, and it had more inviting curb appeal (from the photos).

If a couple sold the Larchmont house and moved to Bethlehem, they could enjoy comparable living space, but with a major financial improvement. Even assuming the Larchmont home still had a quarter million dollar mortgage, after the broker's commission, the sellers would clear $435,000. That's enough to buy the house in Bethlehem for cash and still have $120,000 left over. That sum invested in U.S. Treasury securities would yield about $6,000 a year (as of early 2007), plus the new Bethlehem residents would be living mortgage-free. Property taxes, home owner's insurance, and auto insurance premiums would also decline.

The move, of course, means a totally different lifestyle. With New York just under two hours by car, it's not a drive you would make every day, but visiting friends and family in metro New York would not be difficult. It may mean finding a new set of medical professionals and a new church, but it also means making new friends and discovering new places. It offers a more relaxed pace, and has fewer financial pressures than life in the fast lane of the Big Apple.

For Boomers on a budget, these kinds of in-region moves are possible in many metropolitan areas. In most cases, you don't have to go a full two hours out of a major city to find relative bargains. While this type of move involves some sacrifices, it allows Boomers to unlock value stored in their homes, and use it to reduce debt, improve income, and enjoy more day-to-day activities. For those who no longer need to trek into a city every day to make a living, why pay a housing premium for the convenience of city access, and the high taxes that go along with prime suburban property?

RELOCATE

This is the big move. It means selling your longstanding residence and making a major migration. It is probably an airplane ride away from the old stomping grounds. It can be as short as three to four hours by car, but it's not a one-day round-trip drive. This is for people who weighed all the benefits of staying close to home versus the gains to be won by making a move, and pulled the trigger. They are the "equity bandits," cashing in their chips and heading out of town, dragging their suburban or big city equity with them.

Yes, they want the money that was locked up in their home, but there is more going on here. The "relocators" want a better climate, different scenery, a new adventure. They might be moving for an employment opportunity. Their children may be spread out already, leaving less incentive to stay put. They may have moved several times over the last 15 or 20 years, and don't feel deeply rooted in a particular community.

They may be moving to connect with old friends or an old flame. They may be yearning for a fresh start and a new lifestyle. Perhaps they had a wonderful vacation somewhere and always thought it would be a great place to live. They may have been dreaming about a condo on a golf course or fishing for trout in a country stream for decades, and now is their time. Americans have a long history of moving for new opportunities, and some Boomers will carry on that tradition as they approach their retirement years. With email, cheap telephone rates, and low-cost airfares, a long distance move is not exactly like heading down the Oregon Trail by wagon train.

"One thing the Boomers have going for them is their real estate. Real estate to the rescue," says Fred Brock, author of *Retire on Less Than You Think*. "And you are seeing that happen all over the country as Boomers are . . . moving to places where they can buy a house outright and not have a mortgage payment—or if they don't buy it outright, they at least have enough of a down payment that their mortgage becomes incidental to their expenses, and makes their lifestyle much cheaper."

The great escape has a romantic lure, but also poses some challenges. It may mean starting out with few, if any, friends, adjusting to a different culture and political climate, and finding reliable medical and personal service professionals. It's critical to investigate the quality of health care facilities in the area. The local news media may be an eye-popping disappointment, so make sure high-speed Internet access is available. Inquire about any large developments that are being planned, which could spoil the character of the community. And if you have a taste for fine dining, don't be shocked if the local establishments leave you hankering for home.

If you plan to move to an area that is dramatically different from what you have known, it may be wise to rent for a year while you adjust to the new territory. Even if you are smitten by the spectacular countryside and local charm, give yourself time to get acclimated. If you venture from Manhattan to Mayberry, there may be a few too many Barney Fifes for your taste. In recent years, some who moved from the Northeast to Florida discovered it was not for them, and moved part way back to their home region. They're known as "half-backs" and they're fueling the popularity of communities in the Carolinas. The point is, avoid an expensive real estate transaction until you know it's a keeper. Unless you are sure you have found paradise, have an easy exit plan at the ready.

WHERE THE BUFFALO ROAM

As an advocate for selling the high-priced plot in suburbia and heading for the low-cost hinterlands, journalist Fred Brock is walking the talk. He and his wife moved from a New Jersey suburb of New York City to Manhattan, Kansas, where he teaches at Kansas State University. (Fred's story is presented in detail in chapter 11. His move was not only a financial bonanza, but a lifestyle success as well. "Now, is it a perfect match? Not necessarily," says Fred. "There are things I miss about New York. There are no sushi restaurants. There are no Japanese restaurants in Manhattan [Kansas], and I love sushi. But the barbecue's great, the lifestyle is excellent, the air's clean, the cost of living is good...and I particularly like to bicycle and it's wonderful to bicycle here. The Flint Hills are full of these wonderful bicycle trails and roads that are fabulous.

"From a fast-paced urban lifestyle, we've come to a much slower lifestyle, and it's wonderful," says Fred. "I mean, you can leave New York and come to a place where the buffalo roam, and I think that's the kind of thing we're going to see the Boomers doing as time goes by."

And, yes, it was Fred's move to Kansas that Dee Lee was commenting on earlier in this chapter. A prime example of how the choice between staying put and picking up stakes depends on your worldview and your very personal circumstances.

COMBO PLATE

"I'll have the combo plate." That's what Boomers are saying who want to age in place *and* have a second home for periodic getaways. Many Boomers already have a second home. A study for the Research Institute for Housing America said that, as of 2004, of the 43 million U.S. households comprised of individuals age 50 and over who owned a principal residence, about 15 percent also owned a second home. Second-home ownership rises sharply with education, with almost one-quarter of fifty-plus home owner college graduates having a second home.

Because of the size of the Boomer generation, the number of second homes is forecast to grow by two million over the next 10 years. The Hanley Wood study, cited earlier, said 44 percent of the "Boomfluentials" surveyed want to build, buy, or rent a second home so they can live in two different areas. "One of the things that has been surprising about Boomers," says economist Chip Case, "is that they look at housing the way we think of television sets or cars. They don't own one; sometimes it's two or three."

The combo plate allows Boomers to enjoy the benefits of being based in their longtime communities, while having the chance to relax and have fun in a vacation setting. The second home may also be large enough to accommodate visitors, and can be used by family members for their own getaways. Surveys indicate that about one Boomer in eight plans to sell his main residence and move to his second home. Some housing experts cite examples where Boomers have sold a large house, moved to a condo within their home community, and used the remaining sale proceeds to buy a vacation home. They own the same square footage, just split between two houses.

Second home hot spots look like an array of posters on a travel agency wall. The most popular include Florida, North Carolina's Outer Banks, northern New England, the Adirondacks, northern areas of Michigan, Wisconsin, and Minnesota, the Ozarks, Colorado, and Arizona.

According to the "Housing Trends Among Baby Boomers" study, second homes sit empty most of the time. Half the owners say they spend two weeks or less per year in the second home; only one-third of owners spend a month or more in their second house.

This is an expensive lifestyle, even for Boomers who inherit a mountain retreat or a beachside bungalow. Purchasing a second home is obviously a major outlay, but even maintaining one is costly. Home number two still requires taxes, maintenance, insurance, electricity, telephone, water and sewer expenses, yard work, and possibly heating, cooling, cable TV, and high-speed Internet access. It needs to be furnished and decorated. Travel to and from the house also adds up. It's all a matter of how much money people have and how they want to spend it.

Second home costs may be offset if the property gains in value and can be sold at a profit. If you sell a second home it will be subject to capital gains tax. Mortgage interest on a second home is tax deductible, as long as the total balance of all mortgages on both residences is under $1,000,000 ($500,000 for married filing separately). This assumes the mortgages were taken out after October 13, 1987. Interest on mortgages taken out before that date is also deductible, but may have special tax considerations.

Less costly alternatives include buying a second home with friends or other family members, splitting the expenses, and drawing lots for when the home can be used. Renting a second home may also cost less, and offers the flexibility of spending time in different locations. You can buy a lot of fun with what it costs to keep up a second home. Before buying that second house, get a full picture of what it will cost to purchase and maintain the property, and whether the home will get enough use to justify the expense.

Second homes can also have a strong emotional pull. Some have been in the family for generations. They have been the setting for summer vacations and special gatherings for decades. Boomers may have childhood memories of wonderful times at a family beach house or lakeside cottage, and they want their grandchildren to have the same experience. That's a special place with deep personal meaning. You can't put a price tag on that.

PRESERVE YOUR EQUITY

Much of what we've discussed in this chapter is based on the premise that many Boomers have seen considerable appreciation in property values. It's a good thing, because most of us have not been the most diligent savers. But rising real estate values have tempted Americans to tap into home equity for fleeting lifestyle enhancements such as trips and luxury cars. Some have treated their homes like giant piggy banks that they can't resist raiding. This is generally a bad idea, but is especially risky for Boomers. We just don't have as much time to make up for setbacks as people in their thirties.

Many of us will benefit greatly from selling homes and using those funds to provide for the future. But if you've already consumed most of your home equity and then decide to move, your real estate profits will be meager, and you'll be carrying a hefty new mortgage into old age.

If you are counting on your home to be a long-term investment, don't spend the equity like it's ready cash. As the old saying goes, "My assets are very liquid; they all go down the drain."

7

IT'S YOUR MOVE

While Boomers decide whether to age in place, downsize close to home, or relocate to a new area, the housing choices that express personal tastes, individual dreams, and diverse lifestyles will be the most interesting to watch. What housing options will emerge from a generation known for rewriting the rules? As they have done before, many Boomers will chart their own course, and break from the patterns of prior generations.

Single Boomer women may join in *Golden Girls* housing arrangements. The growing popularity of cohousing may accelerate. Developers are eyeing more college towns to build communities for Boomers, who want to tap into academic and cultural offerings on campus, and be in tune with a young and vibrant atmosphere. Those who share a passion for yoga, meditation, and living a spiritual life can form an "intentional community" to integrate lifestyle with housing. Some Boomers may turn retirement into one big road trip, using new RV condo sites that offer pools and golf courses, in addition to a fully equipped spot to park a luxurious rig.

Many Boomers will follow their parents into active adult communities, but even these developments are undergoing a transformation, with new amenities such as hiking trails and wiring for high-tech home offices. As Boomers prepare to reinvent themselves and redefine aging, a rich variety of housing options is available. From buying a chic city condo to building the perfect country house to moving to a foreign country, this is the time to turn a dream into reality. Let's consider some of the housing options that are emerging. Perhaps, you can find one that fills your needs without emptying your bank account.

ACTIVE ADULT COMMUNITIES

Boomers do not see themselves as old, elder, senior, silver, golden, or retired. They will hang on to a youthful self-image, at least in attitude and lifestyle, long after some of the above descriptions would seem to fit. That outlook has caused builders of "retirement communities" to rebrand their developments as "active adult communities."

"When Del Webb built the first Sun City in Arizona in 1960, most people of that generation expected to live 10 more years after retiring," says Dave Schreiner, vice president of active adult business development for the Del Webb brand of Pulte Homes. "Today, the good news is once you pass from your child-rearing, career-oriented stage of life into this new stage, you might live another 40 years. The possibilities to grow, to experience new things, to get further education, are all in front of you and most people have great zest for that in this stage of their life."

Many empty nest Boomers who are moving into active adult communities are still working, either full-time or part-time. "A large number of Del Webb residents are starting new businesses, getting retrained, and staying connected to the workforce. They don't leave it entirely," says Schreiner. This Boomer work ethic has caused developers to include home offices in design plans and to install extra phone lines and wiring for high-speed Web access. Del Webb reports that in some communities in the western United States, home owners are paying extra to have detached "casitas" built to serve as a home office. Boomer work habits are even affecting decisions on where to build. "That's one advantage of positioning our newer communities close to large metropolitan centers—that's where the jobs are," says Schreiner. "It's quite possible that someday you'll see the first Del Webb community located next to an office park, instead of a shopping mall or medical center."

HOUSING TO MATCH VALUES

Based on the Hanley Wood survey of "Boomfluentials"—home owners ages 50 to 60 with household incomes of $100,000 or more—Boomers prefer very different adult communities than the old model of a golf course snaking through a maze of homes, occupied by mostly older, wealthy, white residents. "Boomfluentials" were asked to respond to a dozen residential community concepts, regardless of whether they would ever consider living there. Here are the themes with the most positive responses:

65 percent: An "outdoor living community" designed for people who love the great outdoors and activities from hiking to biking to nature walks

61 percent: A "Margaritaville community"—a relaxed living community for people who enjoy a laid-back, casual lifestyle

58 percent: A "green community" designed for modern, convenient living without doing damage to the environment

57 percent: A "cultured community" focused on a love of learning, art, music, and the sharing of ideas

56 percent: A "multicultural community" where everyone doesn't look like me

53 percent: A "health community" focused on maintaining whole health through fitness and nutrition

Only **28 percent** responded favorably to a "golfers' community" that caters to the needs and lifestyles of golfers.

The broad strokes of the Hanley Wood survey point to a generation that wants to be physically active and healthy, to live informally and amid diversity, and to live in harmony with the environment. "We all went to summer camp and these are summer camps for the older population," says Wellesley College economist Karl Case, in describing active adult communities. "I'm surprised that the market hasn't responded sooner. But it's responding now."

CREATURE COMFORTS

Boomers moving into active adult communities are often downsizing to just two bedrooms, but they want that smaller space to have a degree of luxury. "Typically they don't need all the space," says Del Webb's Dave Schreiner. "They would like to have all the space they live in—the great room area, the kitchen, the master bedroom—be of high quality and perhaps even nicer than what they had before. But they don't need all those extra bedrooms and maybe they don't need a third garage stall."

Boomers who are empty nesters are looking for a home that matches their new circumstances. "So they want to rightsize their house to fit this new stage of life when it's less about the house and more about the lifestyle that comes with the house," says Schreiner. "They typically need spaces for their hobbies and jobs that they may do. His and hers offices are popular. They are very social, so they like to have a kitchen that's attached to a great room space, but they are still not willing to leave the creature comforts. They like their master bath areas; they like his and hers vanities, nice tubs, walk-in showers; and they like nice counter surface materials. So, they are willing to invest in those areas for their creature comforts, but they are sort of jettisoning those items in the house that really don't fit their lifestyle."

IT'S MY TURN

People are not choosing these developments to retire, but to downsize and have some fun. At a gathering at Caldwell Farm, a fifty-five-plus community north of Boston, resident Linda Bilo put it succinctly: "I've had four children. I've done all that stuff. I am a grandparent. I love it, but it's time for me to start playing again." Active adult communities are working to accommodate the Boomer attitude that life is moving in their direction. They have more time for themselves, and they want housing and amenities that support their new lifestyles.

Many newer communities are creating hiking trails and bike paths, along with the traditional pools, golf courses, and tennis courts. Fitness centers are popular, and many developments are increasing social activities to meet Boomer demands for a greater sense of community. "I think physically we are younger than our parents might have been at this age. So we are looking forward to staying real active," says Caldwell Farm resident Bill McNamara.

Shedding all those suburban home owner responsibilities is also a big draw for the active adult market. Those moving into these communities will be having tag sales to unload their lawn mowers and snowblowers. Tired of all the scraping, painting, and maintenance work he had done on his suburban home, Richard Duncan, and his wife Lillian, moved into Caldwell Farm. Not long after the move, it snowed. "I wanted to see if they had finished the driveway," says Richard. "So I opened the garage door, and somebody was out there spreading salt, and there were three guys shoveling the front walk. I felt a little guilty that I wasn't shoveling, but actually it was pretty good."

FAMILY MATTERS

Polling indicates that about half of Boomers plan to move to a new home for retirement. A Del Webb survey indicates that among those who intend to move, 47 percent say "staying within three hours of family would be an important consideration about where to relocate for retirement." As a result, Del Webb and other active adult developers are building more communities in the Northeast and Midwest. "There's a secret weapon in our business and it's called grandkids," says Dave Schreiner. "For those people who have them...staying close to family and friends, and maintaining links to their community are important things to them. And there are plenty of these 'retire in place' people in markets like Denver, Cleveland, and Detroit."

In choosing Caldwell Farm in Massachusetts, Richard and Lillian Duncan moved only a short distance from the suburban house they had occupied for nearly 20 years. Staying close to family was a big factor in their choice. "Florida to me is a nice place to visit and maybe go for vacation," says Richard. "But at this point, I don't really have any desire to live there. We have three kids up here and we have three grandchildren right now and another on the way. So the thought of not being around them for a long time doesn't seem like something we want to do." Adds Lillian Duncan, "I think with the grandchildren, a week goes by, and I have to see them. So I couldn't move away for a whole winter without seeing them."

One of the issues for Boomers going into active adult communities is whether their move shuts the door on any possibility of an adult child coming home to live with them. Many of these communities have age restrictions that allow younger visitors for just a limited number of days per month. That's fine for occasional visits, but what about boomerang kids in their early twenties who need to come back home after college? For the Duncans, the policy at Caldwell Farm was a big plus. "When we met with the sales manager that was the first question I asked," says Lillian. "Could we have someone, one of our older children, living with us? And he said that they don't discriminate and we could have children living with us if we wanted. That made us feel much better with the decision, knowing that our son is welcome, and that he could live here if he wanted to."

Richard and Lillian Duncan are pleased with their choice. Richard still commutes to his job. Home maintenance is minimal. The children and grandchildren are nearby. For Lillian, it's a sign of progress. "I think that it was so different for our parents' generation. They just lived in the same home—most of them that I know, our friends' parents—and they never thought of doing anything like this. I don't think the concept of town houses, condominium living was available then. It's like—we've raised our children, we've put them through college, and now it's time to do something for us. And this is great. It's social, it's new, it's exciting."

BIG BOOMER ON CAMPUS

Boomers interested in lifelong learning are choosing from a growing number of active adult communities that are linked to colleges and universities. Residents can take classes, use fitness facilities, and attend cultural and athletic events on campus. Some offer discounts at campus dining halls and bookstores. The colleges receive financial benefits from licensing their name, the sale of land for the development, fees for use of campus facilities, and donations from community residents. These communities are especially attractive to alumni, who may want to relive some of their past glory days, and to faculty and staff who want to stay connected to a college or university.

Some of the existing developments are continuing care retirement communities with a high level of services, meal plans, and built-in medical care. These tend to have older residents. Newer developments are targeting the younger Boomer demographic and promoting an active lifestyle with considerable campus interaction. Some communities use a condominium model where residents own their units. Others have an entrance fee, most of which is refundable when residents die or leave the community. All the communities charge a monthly fee for building maintenance and services.

The best of these communities have a strong relationship with the college, and a staff member who assists residents in accessing a wide variety of campus offerings. Residents can find excellent volunteer opportunities in area schools, hospitals, libraries, and cultural institutions. Some residents get directly involved with campus life. For example, a former journalist could be an occasional guest lecturer or mentor staff members of the college newspaper.

Colleges in suburban and rural areas are finding it more difficult to attract students who are seeking the bright lights and excitement of urban campuses. But Boomers are seen as a growth market. By teaming up with developers to create campus-related communities, schools become a magnet for Boomers who want the advantages of being near a college, but are looking for a quieter, less expensive lifestyle. From lectures and book groups to concerts and basketball games, campuses offer a wide variety of interesting, low-cost activities. For Boomers who want to stay physically fit, mentally alert, and engaged in the community, the campus scene may be a great choice. Advocates for campus-related communities envision a national consortium for sharing successful ideas, and a home-exchange network to allow residents from different communities to swap homes for periods of time.

For more information on university-linked retirement communities, check the following resources:

Campus Continuum, at www.campuscontinuum.com, is a company focused on developing, marketing, and operating university-branded fifty-five-plus active adult communities. The site has links to an extensive library of articles on college-linked retirement communities.

Collegiate Retirement Community Consultants, at www.collegiateretirementcommunity.com, focuses on providing a "hands-on advisory" service from initial concept to the first two years of operation of college/university-linked retirement communities.

COHOUSING

When the Met Life Mature Market Institute and AARP asked 500 people ages 50 to 65 if they'd be "interested in building a new home to share with friends that included private space and communal living areas," 22 percent said yes. Advocates of cohousing believe that a significant number of Boomers might prefer to plan their own community with friends or people of similar interests instead of buying into a traditional development. It harkens back to '60s communes, but with contemporary amenities and more privacy. The idea is to consume less, live simply, and share in a community.

The Cohousing Association of the United States lists about 100 active cohousing developments with another 150 at various stages of development. Most cohousing in the United States today is multigenerational, with about one-third of residents over age 55, according to Zev Paiss, a baby Boomer, cohousing consultant, and cofounder of the Elder Cohousing Network. He thinks the cohousing concept is about to take off as Boomers age. "I recently traveled to Florida to meet with developers and to speak to small groups of consumers," says Paiss. "One group of seven couples had originally moved there from the Northeast. They currently lived in gated communities and hated it. They still felt isolated and lonely. But they loved the concept of cohousing, of being able to age with friends, not strangers."

Cohousing homes vary from studio apartments to three-bedroom units, but a typical residence has two floors with a finished basement. The average living space is around 1,200 square feet. Common space allows for day care, guest rooms, group meals, and classes. The emphasis is on close neighbors and shared space. Community members generally share responsibilities for occasional meal preparation or yard work. "Cohousing neighborhoods are created by the residents themselves," says Boulder, Colorado, cohousing advocate Neshama Abraham. "Homes in cohousing are privately owned, and everyone is an equal owner in the shared facilities which include the land, the gardens, and play areas. People share meals together several times a week. It's a neighborhood style, which people are choosing because they want to live more simply, consume less, and have a smaller footprint."

"Boomers are attracted to cohousing because it recreates a sense of community that is important to them," says Zev Paiss. "In some ways it may be similar to an extended family that they grew up with, small towns they might have lived in. It really brings back the importance of the security and safety and the heartfelt beauty of knowing the people you live near."

Initial costs of cohousing are similar to buying a condo or a town house in the same community. It's market rate housing, unless the group decides to subsidize some of the units for low-income residents. Generally, "green" building materials are used, reducing energy consumption. Residents often buy in bulk and travel together to shop. They trade services like babysitting, watering plants, and pet care. Some developments are chosen to be on transit lines, reducing automobile usage.

Boomer couple Dave and Donna Hazen bought into the Wild Sage cohousing development in Boulder about six years ago. "We were living in a five-bedroom suburban house. It wasn't a very satisfying place to be living," says Dave. "The first six to eight weeks we were here, maybe four kids learned to ride a bicycle without training wheels, with a lot of adults standing around applauding. It was really a wonderful experience."

Donna Hazen appreciates the sense of community. "It's just so nice for me. I can chat with my neighbors. The kids here are wonderful, and things happen here, like someone's birthday, so they'll bring a cake out on the common house grounds and people just show up."

Cohousing is a collaborative effort, typically started by a small group. They look for land to buy and hire architects and builders. It generally takes about two years from concept to completion. Even cohousing enthusiasts say it's not for everyone. It takes patience and dedication to make it work, especially during the development stage. There are lots of meetings and details to work out. It's all about building group consensus, not about top-down decision making. Experts say certain personality types tend to do well with this process: teachers, mental health workers, artists, writers, and others who see themselves as self-starters.

"The best size community to aim for is 20 to 40 households," says consultant Zev Paiss. "Some of the newer cohousing developments are age-restricted to people over 55. One of the first was Silver Sage here in Boulder, my hometown." Silver Sage is adjacent to Wild Sage, a mixed cohousing development. Both are part of a new mixed-use neighborhood, which is designed to avoid isolation, and provide communal life with privacy and access to a larger, more diverse community.

"Each cohousing complex has its own character and amenities," says Paiss. "Glacier Circle in California has built a caregiver's apartment for a nurse so there will be someone there 24/7 who can help when residents become ill. Others have hired a professional chef to cook several meals a week."

"I think the appeal to Boomers for cohousing, whether it's age-specific or multigenerational, is that it's a chance to reinvent how you are going to live in the second phase of your life," says Neshama Abraham. "When you are in a cohousing model it's so easy for you to be there for each other, to have a neighbor that you check on, or someone checks on you. That's what cohousing is about. It's a lifestyle that allows someone to age in community."

Information on cohousing is available from the Cohousing Association of the United States, at www.cohousing.org.

BUILD YOUR DREAM HOUSE

When the last of the children are out of the house, it's an opportunity, possibly for the first time in your life, to design and create the exact living space you have always wanted. For all the cramped kitchens, misplaced closets, dank laundry rooms, and odd floor plans that you have endured, now is the time to set the world right. That means building your dream house from the ground up.

For Tobey Pierce and Anne Winter, that meant constructing a 2,300 square foot wooded retreat on a bluff above the Potomac River in West Virginia. It's only about 75 miles from the three-story row house in Washington, D.C., where they raised four children, but it might as well be on another planet. It is a quiet, secluded spot that is close to nature and in harmony with the retirement life they envision.

The process of building a house begins long before the ground-breaking. It starts in the mind. "Anne and I started talking about what was most important in our lives," says Tobey. "Wouldn't it be nice to actually have a place where we could have a big garden, and where we could get dogs that like to run around? Living in nature has a tremendous value for both of us. Having privacy, being able to appreciate views. Having coffee in the morning, where you can just walk out with a cup of coffee and there you'd be in the middle of the woods. We wanted a house where we felt good."

With an image of their ideal setting in mind, Tobey and Anne looked for the right location, which they found northwest of Washington, D.C., where the Potomac River forms the border between West Virginia and Maryland. "I knew when I saw this place that this was it," says Anne. "It's just a breathtaking place." Tobey says the beauty of the location helped to inspire the design. "The place itself had this really strong attraction when we saw it, and we tried to build a house that lived up to the space," he says.

The couple hired acclaimed architect Mark McInturff to design a home that was practical and beautiful, and which fit naturally into the stunning riverside setting. The final design was a two-story central building with living room and kitchen downstairs, and a master suite on the second floor. Big windows open up spectacular views of the countryside. A screened porch connects the main house to a guest wing that includes a bath and sleeping loft. On the opposite side, a corridor connects the main building to a cozy study with fireplace. And of course, they have the beautiful garden and a couple of frolicking dogs, just as they had imagined.

In creating a house that would take them into the future, Tobey and Anne drew upon the past. From childhood memories to their everyday use of space, their experience shaped the design of their dream house. "A lot of the houses that we've lived in, the limitations of those houses, have helped steer the design of this house," says Anne. "In our house in Washington the kitchen was away, and when we had people over, I felt like I was missing the party if I was in the kitchen cooking. So now, we have the kitchen as the center, and I can participate in the conversation while I am cooking."

"I grew up in a house in Connecticut, and it had a screen porch breezeway, and so we put in a screen porch breezeway," says Tobey. "It was a wonderful part of my life growing up as a young boy, and it's now part of my life as I'm older. My grandparents had a house with clapboards so we wanted to do that as well. I love stone and you can see around you, we have a huge stone terrace here. We have a stone chimney. The stone has a wonderful sort of eternal quality to it, a solidness to it."

The house is designed for the life of its occupants. The kitchen and living room are at the center. The study is a media room with computer. Anne does yoga in the quiet of the master bedroom. Though not a large home, it has ample privacy. "We don't have four bedrooms," says Tobey. "We have basically our bedroom and a guest bedroom and that's it. It's all anybody really needs when you are a so-called empty nester. We wanted a house that we could live in throughout the various seasons. When it's very hot in the summer and there are bugs, we hang out in the screened porch. During the fall and the spring, we sit out on the patio, which has such fantastic views. In the winter, we have a cozy little room with a woodstove, so we hang out in there."

After many years devoted to family and career in an urban setting, Tobey and Anne have a new life and a dream house in the country. "We used everything we could from the site," says Tobey, "the trees, the stone, the view, the topography, and we created what we believe is something that we've always wanted."

Looking out over the trees to the water below, Anne has the last word: "It's just a wonderful place to be."

AVOID THE HOME-BUILDING BLUES

Building a home is a complicated process that can be filled with conflicts, frustrations, disappointments, and unexpected costs. A few key steps can lower the risk of having your dream home turn into a house of horrors.

Envision. They call it a dream house, so dream! Take a lot of time to visualize what you want in your house. Talk for hours with your spouse or partner. Where will it be located? How big will it be? What architectural style do you want? What rooms do you want? What improvements can you make from prior homes you have lived in? How will the house complement your lifestyle?

Using inexpensive home design software, make some of your own drawings and play around with design ideas. You may gain some insights that will help when you are ready to talk to a professional designer.

Location. In looking for home sites, consider these factors:

- Employers: Will you keep your current job or be looking for work?
- Transportation
- Medical facilities, shops, public safety services, library
- Schools: Maybe not an issue for you, but it could affect value if you ever sell.
- Utilities
- Water/sewer
- Internet access
- Neighbors: Try to meet the neighbors, to avoid unpleasant surprises later on.

- Noise
- Potential development in the area
- Suitability for building: Heavily wooded plots or those with rocky ledges and hilly terrain can cost more to prepare for construction.
- Zoning and permits

Cost. How much house can you afford to build? Before hiring an architect, you need to know your budget. Generally, people building homes get a construction loan for the building period, and then pay that off with a conventional mortgage. You may be using prior home equity to pay for some, and possibly all, of the construction. Run all the numbers to determine how much you can spend on your dream house.

One way to get a feel for what your home will cost is to look at several new homes in the area where you want to build. Check the price and square footage of those homes. Subtract from the home prices the estimated cost of land, and you can roughly calculate the price per square foot of new construction in that locale. For example, let's say you look at a 2,200 square foot house that costs $300,000. If the building site is worth $30,000, then the cost of constructing the new house was around $123 per square foot ($270,000/2,200). If you do this with a few houses and take an average price per square foot, you'll have a good idea how much your house will cost, assuming it is not radically different from those in your sample.

The most expensive rooms per square foot are usually the kitchen and baths. If you have grandiose plans for those rooms, you will have to factor that into your budget.

A two-story home will have a lower cost per square foot than a long, rambling one-story house because the roof and foundation cover a smaller area. Plumbing and ventilation systems can also be installed at lower cost in the more compact space.

Design. You may hire an architect at this point, or a builder who will hire all the other key players including a designer. In either case, get references and check out their work. Have a clear understanding of what is expected in the design contract: scope of the work, cost, timetable, and role of the designer during the construction phase.

Do not pick a design until you have purchased the land. The topography and surroundings will have a bearing on the design. Many ready-made house plans are available for sale, or your designer may be able to save you money by customizing an existing plan to fit your needs.

Build. Choosing the right contractor is critical. It may not be the one with the best price. This relationship will be tested, so you need someone who is thorough, professional, and a good communicator. If the builder has too much of a "back of the envelope" approach, it will probably lead to trouble down the road when changes are made, schedules are broken, and disagreements arise.

Scrutinize the builder's contract. This document is the foundation of your business arrangement, and a lot of money is riding on a successful relationship. Before signing, ask questions about any aspect that seems confusing. Ask yourself the "what if" questions. Imagine things that could go wrong, and see how the contract applies. If you are not satisfied, insist on language that will work. Putting adequate thought and planning into the process up front will save you headaches and dollars later on.

During construction, visit the site regularly. Communicate frequently with the builder. Ask questions and write down the answers. Take copious notes and keep neat files. Put dates on all documents. Save receipts, model numbers, paint chips, carpet samples, etc.

Don't forget landscaping. That may involve moving around a lot of dirt and rocks, and planting trees, shrubs, and grass. Will fencing be required? Is there a paved driveway? Outdoor patio? Exterior lighting? Make sure you have all these in your budget.

Two critical areas are changes and cost overruns. As construction progresses, many owners ask for changes. These invariably raise the price of the project. Discuss what changes will cost before making your decision. If you eliminate an item, discuss how that will reduce costs. Experts suggest that you be prepared for the house to cost up to 10 percent more than the original estimate.

The builder is doing the heavy lifting, but the owner also has a big job of oversight and staying actively engaged in the project. That can end up saving money, and getting what is most important: the house of your dreams.

HASTA LA VISTA, BABY

Boomer couple Dan Prescher and Suzan Haskins are a long way from home, or what used to be home. One too many frigid Nebraska winters sent them packing south of the border, first to Quito, Ecuador, and then to San Miguel de Allende, Mexico. Located in the mountainous region of Central Mexico, San Miguel de Allende has attracted a lively North American community. Famous for its mild climate, colonial architecture, and vibrant arts scene, San Miguel de Allende has an expatriate population of some 6,000 to 8,000, the majority of whom are Americans.

Dan and Suzan are not actually retired. When they moved in 2001, they changed careers. They had a successful public relations and marketing business in Omaha, but after many memorable vacations in Mexico and Central America, they felt a strong pull southward. "Every winter we'd just look at ourselves and say, 'Never another winter in Nebraska,'" says Dan. "Fortunately, we were in a place where a lot of Boomers are, where we could afford to fail gracefully if we tried something different."

They closed the business, sold their house and cars (but kept the dog), and went to work for International Living, which offers publications and consulting services for Americans relocating to foreign countries. By late 2001, they were living in Quito, the capital of Ecuador, nearly 10,000 feet up in the Andes Mountains. They spent the rest of that year and the next exploring, writing, and hosting International Living subscribers in South America.

If the polling data is correct, several million Boomers may join Dan and Suzan in living outside the United States for at least some period in their lives. In the Wood Hanley housing survey of affluent Boomers, 12 percent of those polled said they were "very" or "somewhat" likely to move to another country within the next 10 to 15 years.

In late 2002, International Living decided to open an office in Mexico and Dan and Suzan jumped at the chance to run the operation. In an article about the expat life in Mexico, Dan and Suzan describe the pleasures of San Miguel de Allende:

> "For people like us, it's perfect. We can have all the adventure, warm weather, and south-of-the-border charm we want without giving up a thing. We can sit in quaint village plazas and have tacos for lunch, and then we can get on the phone or the Internet and catch up on news from friends and family. We can walk to weekly street markets for fruits, vegetables, and handicrafts, or we can visit a Sam's Club, Costco, Home Depot, or Office Max if we need to. We can take a two-day ride on horseback into the mountains to visit archeological sites covered with ancient hieroglyphs, or we can fly from just about anywhere in Mexico back to the U.S. in just a couple of hours."

The couple bought a five-bedroom house with a spacious yard in a quiet neighborhood of San Miguel de Allende. Two of the rooms serve as offices. They have no mortgage. With the temperate climate, utility costs are negligible, and they pay property taxes of just $300 a year. "It's extremely affordable," says Dan. "People can come down here and start looking [for homes] at $150,000, and then you can go up as high as you want."

Named after a hero in the war for independence from Spain, San Miguel de Allende is a beautiful city with narrow cobblestone streets, ornate cathedrals, and colorful galleries and shops. "We have seen people who have come down here who have been so worried about what they are going to do in their retirement," says Suzan. "And they find there are so many opportunities and so many great things to do.

They are taking painting classes and acting workshops and writing workshops, and they are able to reawaken those old interests that they had long ago."

Though the American expatriate community is sizable, Dan Prescher recommends breaking out of that comfort zone to experience the authentic Mexico. "Foreigners will move down here and just bunch up and keep to themselves. There are people who have lived here for 20 years and have never bothered to learn the language, simply because they don't have to. You can get by with English down here. But I don't know why you would do that. I don't know why you would come to a country like this with a culture like this, and not at least try to learn the language and participate a little bit, because it's fascinating and it's a show of respect."

During a night of fireworks celebrating Mexican independence, we had a camera crew for the *Boomers!* television series videotaping in the main square of San Miguel de Allende. Several American expats talked about living in this charming old Mexican city. "The people who have been drawn to San Miguel are people who are artistic," said Warren Hardy. "They are people interested in all sorts of arts and in mental stimulus, and continued learning."

"We like everything about it here," said Adam Mitchell. "The intellectual life is great. The weather is fantastic. The air is clean; you can always see for 50 miles. There are so many interesting things to do."

Linda Whynman and her husband Saul were enjoying the festivities. "There is a tremendous amount of creativity down here," observed Linda. "There's a tremendous amount of enthusiasm and giving and volunteerism, and um, good sex." Saul burst out laughing, and agreed, "The sex is wonderful. I wake up every morning and say, 'I love Mexico.'"

FIELD GUIDE TO LIVING OVERSEAS

If you are contemplating a move to a foreign country, get ready to do your homework in advance and be prepared for a culture shock once you get there. "It's easier to stay at home, and often more comfortable, and certainly more convenient," says Suzan Haskins, who is Latin American editorial director for *International Living* magazine. "But there is much to gain from other cultures, and you will learn that the world is full of wonderful, amazing people."

Here are some tips on living overseas from Suzan and the experts at *International Living*:

Tax planning. Before moving to another country, consult with tax attorneys both in the U.S. and in your destination country. Get a clear understanding of how income from employment, pensions, Social Security, interest, dividends, and capital gains will be taxed. If you intend to buy property, find out about property and excise taxes.

Language. To get a fuller appreciation of a foreign country, learn the language, or as much of it as you can. If you know the language, you will end up having more meaningful experiences and interactions with people. If you have a medical condition, carry an index card describing your situation written in the local language. "In many places you will find English speakers," says Suzan. "But the best way to assimilate into your new life is to learn to talk to the locals."

Six-month rule. Many experts recommend spending at least six months in a country before committing to moving there. It is easy to be swept up in the beauty and charm of a community during a short, carefree visit. But you don't know what it would be like to live there until you have experienced a longer stretch during different seasons. Use this time to meet as many expatriates as possible to learn from their experiences. Research what permits and paperwork are needed to become a resident, and make local contacts that can help if you eventually want to buy property. Many countries have affordable lawyers who specialize in expat visas.

Health. Medicare and most U.S. health insurance plans do not cover you in a foreign country. Health insurance is probably available locally at a fraction of what it costs in the United States. Aside from insurance, investigate the quality and availability of health care services. You can always come back to the U.S. for surgery or to see specialists.

Buying property. Getting credit and buying property is easier in the United States than anywhere else in the world. It is often more complicated overseas. Look at several properties, even if you love the first one you see. Be prepared to negotiate. Hire a local real estate attorney (not the same one representing a seller). Insist on title insurance, to make sure ownership is clear and that there are no liens against the property.

Communications. Set up a permanent postal address where all your essential mail can be sent to and from, and where it can be forwarded to you in your new home country. Consider a VOIP (voice over Internet protocol) telephone number. "We use both Vonage and Skype," says Suzan. "Our friends, family, and business associates can call us anytime here in Mexico—for free—via our 800 Vonage number, and it costs us less than $40/month."

Finances. Arrange to do as much online banking and bill paying as possible. Banks in foreign countries may ask for more proof of local residency to set up an account than you would encounter in the U.S. Telephone and utility bills with a local address will help. Be prepared to operate with credit cards and ATM withdrawals from your U.S. accounts.

Culture shock. "No matter how many times you may have visited a country, you won't be prepared for actually living there," says Suzan Hoskins. "Don't expect to find your favorite brands of comfort food on the grocery store shelves. Don't expect things to work the same way they do at home. And when they don't, please don't let it upset you. Plan for power, water, cable TV, and Internet outages. On the other hand, learn to embrace new customs, eat new food, and live life at a slower pace. Remember why you wanted to move there in the first place."

Finally, Suzan cautions not to get overly upset at any initial setbacks. "During our first two months in Ecuador we were in panic mode," she says. "'Oh my God, what have we done?' was our most-used phrase. We soon learned that nearly everyone who moves abroad experiences similar anxiety." Give it time, and you will adjust.

For more on preparing for life in a foreign country, visit the *International Living* website at www.internationalliving.com.

Retiring to Paradise

Bill Shank and Scott D'Appell made a dramatic move, from the fast lane of the New York City arts scene to the tranquil island of Vieques off the coast of Puerto Rico. In his early sixties, Bill is retired after a long career in commercial design and as garden editor for Martha Stewart, where he worked on television shows, magazines, books, and products related to gardening.

Now in his early fifties, Scott was director of education for the Horticultural Society of New York, a position that was eliminated when funding dried up after the 9/11 attacks. He landed a horticulture position on St. Croix in the Virgin Islands.

Bill and Scott had vacationed on Vieques for years. When Bill retired at age 60, they bought land on Vieques and built a home, which they had designed. They described to us their odyssey from New York to Vieques, and how their lives have changed.

Boomers: How did you choose Vieques for your new home?
Bill: We came down here to Vieques 10 years ago on a whim. One day we heard about the island and the next day we decided we'd come. We had no idea where we were going! I always hated hot weather so I thought this might be a big mistake! But we had a *wonderful* two weeks. The next year when it came time for vacation, we did the same thing again. And we came over Thanksgiving. We did that for five years.

(continued)

Retiring to Paradise *(continued)*

Boomers: What would you say to Americans who are thinking of retiring or moving here?

Bill: In New York, we thought, if you're going to retire, you have to have a lot of money. People are afraid. They want to live in gated communities. But here, you're not going to starve because you can eat bananas, you can eat mangoes, you know everything from nature is around you! So there's no fear about retiring down here. And on some days, if you get frustrated with something about island life, you just go down to the beach and say, "God this is beautiful. Why didn't I do this 10 years ago?"

Scott: Well, Bill's retired, but I'm not, and when you live in the Caribbean, nobody has a full-time job. You might work in a bank, you might be the checkout girl in the grocery store, you might work in the pharmacy or the hardware store or be in politics, but there's no full-time job. When you live in the Caribbean, you have to multitask, so I write articles, I write books, but I also sell food and I cater parties. I do garden consultations and I sell plants and when I get my chickens, I will sell eggs. When I get the vegetable garden in, I'll sell fancy produce to the fancy restaurants. All of this to make money! It's a whole other kind of life. It's not stateside at all. It's being very Bohemian!

Boomers: Do you ever miss the lifestyle or conveniences in the States?

Bill: It's a very different life down here and if you come to this island and think, "I want to be the person I was in New York and be very efficient," forget it, because it's not going to happen! We live on an island, and everything comes over on a little ferry. The ferry system is dismal, to put it lightly! If there's a bad storm, we don't have food. The stores are empty. And if there's a strike somewhere, we don't have food or gasoline.

(continued)

Retiring to Paradise

It's just a different culture. We're guests, basically, on the island and once you learn more about the people, I think your life becomes richer and richer. We've gotten involved in some community things and give our time and our experience. Scott lectures locally and I've been involved in a few projects. If you come down here and expect to be entertained, forget it. Because there are no movies, we don't even have a television set; there's no theater, no bowling alley, no decent grocery stores.

Scott: You become nonmaterialistic. You leave all of that behind! Everything you own either rots, rusts, decomposes, or gets eaten. So what you loved, you lose. It's very...cathartic. It's part of paradise. I don't care if I ever see another magnolia or daffodil again! Nor do I care to talk about them, so the fact that I have a whole new realm of Caribbean plants to learn about and to play with and to propagate and to teach people about and to write about, it's fantastic! I don't want to change a thing! I don't want to go up north again; there's nothing there for me anymore. It's a total life change.

Part Four

MONEY

8

BOOMER GUIDE TO THE BASICS OF INVESTING

Most of us never learned in school what has become a new requirement for citizenship in the 21st century. And we don't mean learning how to download songs onto an iPod. No, the new "life skill" that ordinary working Americans are supposed to master is to be a pension fund manager. If you have a 401(k) or similar retirement plan at work, then you're the manager of your own pension. Ready or not, we're a nation of amateur Warren Buffetts. This may seem about as good an idea as having people perform appendectomies on themselves, but that is what we've got, so we better learn to do it right.

This chapter spells out in plain English the key steps for putting together an investment portfolio, whether for a retirement plan at work, for an IRA, or a regular investment account. The next chapter explains how to put these principles to work to get the most out of your 401(k).

DESIGNING YOUR PORTFOLIO

We are going to focus on three main categories of investing: stocks, bonds, and cash. Of course, many other investment options exist, but these are the three main building blocks, and the choices most widely available in retirement plans at work. How you mix these three categories together is what the financial textbooks call "asset allocation." We are trying to keep financial jargon to a minimum, but asset allocation is one of those fundamentals upon which everything else is built.

In fact, choosing your asset allocation is the most important decision you make as an investor. Picking your actual investments has less impact on portfolio performance than on how you divide your account between stocks, bonds, and cash. Generally, if you have more stocks, your returns will be higher over the long term, but you'll also experience more volatility. With stocks, you get more severe ups and downs, but you get paid for your worries with better returns.

Most retirement plans offer mutual funds rather than individual stocks or bonds, so we will concentrate on how to select the right funds. Mutual funds pool together money from many investors, and buy large portfolios of dozens, or hundreds, of stocks or bonds. Each shareholder owns a tiny slice of the portfolio, with his or her money spread over all the investments in the fund.

There are many types of mutual funds, each focusing on a particular segment of the investment universe. For example, funds can invest in large, small, or midsize U.S. stocks, international stocks, a variety of bonds, and several types of cash investments. Some funds are very aggressive, some take moderate risk, while others deliver more safety than growth.

Having so many fund choices may seem bewildering, but it's a little like a symphony orchestra. As you look up at the stage, you see a wide variety of instruments, each of which has a specific role to play. Just as each instrument makes its own sound, each mutual find has a specific purpose in a portfolio. Your job as conductor is to select which funds are right for you, and to have them work together harmoniously to meet your retirement savings goals. It's no piece of cake, but it's a lot easier than learning to play the violin.

STOCK ESSENTIALS

With a stock, you own a slice of a company. If the company succeeds, you should, too. With a stock mutual fund, you essentially own a tiny slice of dozens, or even hundreds, of companies. Owning a single stock concentrates risk in that one company. If it turns out to be a wild success, that's great. But, if it's a clunker, you could lose the entire investment. Owning a mutual fund gives you more "diversification" because it spreads the risk over many companies. It's as simple as the old adage "Don't put all your eggs in one basket."

Mutual funds have highly trained managers to do research and select stocks. The funds send out periodic reports listing which stocks the fund holds, and showing how the fund has performed compared to similar types of investments. Most funds have websites where you can check on your account, and buy and sell shares. Funds charge a management fee, which is deducted from the fund's holdings. The size of that fee is an important factor in choosing a fund. High fees eat away at your returns.

VIVE LA DIFFERENCE

Companies come in all sizes, from privately owned sole proprietorships, which are often a one-person business, to giant publicly traded conglomerates like General Electric with 316,000 employees. Even among companies that issue publicly traded stock there are small, midsize, and large corporations. Size is based on a company's "market capitalization," or "market cap." The market cap is the price of the stock times the number of shares outstanding. In other words, if you were to buy every share of stock in the company, the total price would be its market capitalization.

A large cap company might be worth tens of billions of dollars. A small cap company might be valued at $300 million to $1 billion. Mid caps are somewhere in between. The significance to investors is that large, small, and mid cap stocks tend to go up and down at different rates, at different times. There are periods when large caps are leading the way, and stretches when small or mid caps are in favor. Of course, there are times when all three categories are going down, but at different rates of decline.

Mutual funds tend to concentrate investments in one of the three size categories. Some funds are large cap, some are small cap, and some are mid cap. A well-diversified portfolio includes funds from all three categories. As you increase the variety of investments in your portfolio, each with its own pattern of behavior, you reduce the impact of any one class of investments. You dilute the impact of extreme highs and lows in each category. While that cuts down the gains from a hot sector, it also reduces losses from investments that are tanking. Keeping losses under control is a key to hanging in there during a nasty bear market; having a diverse mix of investments is the key to managing losses.

SIZING THINGS UP

Large U.S. corporations are the most established businesses in the U.S., companies like ExxonMobil, Bank of America, and Procter & Gamble. Companies such as these make up the Standard & Poor's 500, a popular stock index measuring the performance of 500 of the largest U.S. corporations. The S&P 500 is a better guide to large cap performance than the widely known Dow Jones Industrial Average, which has just 30 stocks. Many mutual fund companies offer an S&P 500 Index fund, which provides returns in line with the overall performance of these 500 companies. However, most stock funds are "actively managed," meaning the fund manager picks stocks to buy and sell, and tries to beat the S&P 500 Index. Few fund managers are able to consistently beat the S&P 500 Index over long periods, in part because the costs of having a research staff, paying transaction fees, and servicing shareholders eat away at returns.

As a rule, stock prices of large companies are more stable than for smaller stocks. The big companies are mature and usually not growing rapidly; they are also not likely to go out of business any time soon, though in this changing world economy, no company can be complacent about its future. Most of these corporate giants return some of their profits to shareholders as dividends, paid out each quarter. Over many years, dividends can be a significant portion of your return.

While large stock funds attract the most investment dollars, adding a small stock fund into the mix can add zip to the portfolio. Small companies are often in a more formative stage than are their big brothers. That can mean spurts of rapid growth, or periods of nerve-wracking setbacks. Stocks of smaller companies tend to be more volatile than those of big companies. Because of that added risk, small company stocks have historically offered a higher return than large stocks. This is not true every year, but over 5- or 10-year time periods, small stocks generally do better.

Because small cap stocks behave differently than large caps, mixing the two gives you added diversification, which helps to reduce volatility. An index called the Russell 2000 is a widely followed proxy for small company stock performance. Russell 2000 Index funds match the overall performance of the small cap sector.

Mid caps offer another investment category. Most large cap stocks graduated from mid cap status at some point in their history. Some of today's mid caps will be tomorrow's goliaths. The S&P Mid Cap 400 Index measures the overall performance of medium-size companies. Again, adding this segment to your investment mix gives you a chance to benefit from companies that are expanding, while also increasing your diversification. You can never eliminate all the bumps in the road, but you can smooth your investment ride with a well-constructed, diversified portfolio.

MARCHING TO THEIR OWN DRUMMERS

Below are the annual percentage returns of the S&P 500 Large Cap Index, the S&P Mid Cap 400 Index, and the Russell 2000 Small Cap Index for 10 years, from 1996 to 2005. The decade encompasses the historic market run-up of the late 1990s, the market collapse in 2000 to 2002, and three years of recovery. The numbers show how differently these three market segments behave most of the time:

	1996	1997	1998	1999	2000	2001	2002	2003	2004	2005
S&P 500	22.96	33.36	28.58	21.04	–9.11	–11.89	–22.10	28.68	10.88	4.91
S&P Mid Cap 400	19.06	32.00	18.91	14.54	17.44	–.64	–14.43	35.34	16.35	12.47
Russell 2000	16.49	22.36	–2.55	21.26	–3.02	2.49	–20.48	47.25	18.33	4.55

You can see how large caps led the bull market in 1996 to 1999. Small caps were out of favor in 1998 with a 2.55 percent loss, while large companies ran up a huge 28.58 percent gain. Over time, the large cap sector got overpriced, and when the correction came, it was a case of "the bigger they are, the harder they fall." While large caps were down over 9 percent in 2000, the mid caps were gaining more than 17 percent.

When people talk about how the stock market is doing, they usually mean the Dow Jones Industrials or the S&P 500. However, as you can see, there isn't one market, but many themes and trends working concurrently. The best move is to spread your investments over all three categories to manage the volatility that leaps off the page with this chart.

Size Matters

Here's an example of how a small stock can act very differently from a big one, even within the same industry. Let's say the economy is slowing and the big automobile companies are selling fewer vehicles. Profits are likely to drop at GM and Ford. But, imagine that a small company has just developed a new technology for deploying air bags more safely and at lower cost. Even as the auto industry slumps, the small air bag company enjoys a huge jump in business as it sells to automakers that still need to install millions of air bags. The stock may rise considerably, even as the auto industry pulls into the breakdown lane. If you owned stock in both GM and the small company, your losses at GM would be at least partially offset by gains from the air bag maker. That's diversification in action.

YOU GOTTA HAVE STYLE

In addition to size, stock mutual funds also follow strategies based on the investment styles of growth, value, or blend.

Growth stocks are companies that are growing more rapidly than the overall market. They are high-priced relative to their current profits, but investors are betting that future earnings will be so strong that the stock price will keep moving higher.

However, if the company stumbles, shareholders feel the pain. If you read the financial press or watch business shows on TV, you will occasionally hear about a stock that plunged because of an "earnings disappointment." Those are usually growth companies whose heady profits started to flatten. With a slower growth rate, the market quickly decides that the stock no longer warrants a premium price.

Growth-oriented mutual funds have portfolios dominated by growth stocks. By holding stocks of many companies, funds buffer themselves against steep losses if one company hits the skids. Nevertheless, these funds are more aggressive than the average mutual fund, and are more likely to have steeper gains and declines.

Value stocks are priced modestly relative to their current profits, and the market does not think those profits are likely to grow very rapidly. The company may be in an industry going through sluggish times. It could be that the company is not well managed, that its product line needs revamping, or that it has had legal or regulatory problems.

For some investors, this land of "Rodney Dangerfield stocks" (they get no respect) is fertile ground for discovering opportunities. A company may have better prospects than the marketplace realizes. New management, a new product line, changing economic trends, and the possibility of being a takeover candidate are all factors that could boost the price of a poke-along value stock.

Some investors prefer value stocks because they are less volatile than their flashy growth-style cousins. Since the market has low expectations of these companies, and since their stock prices are already low, they are less likely to drop sharply if there is bad news about the company, or the direction of the overall market. Value-oriented mutual funds focus on these types of companies, constantly searching out diamonds in the rough. If a value fund manager is good at unearthing undervalued gems, fund investors can get a good return without the volatility of a growth fund.

Some mutual funds invest in both growth- and value-oriented stocks, without either category dominating the portfolio. These are **blend funds**. An S&P 500 Index fund is a blend fund because the stocks comprising the S&P 500 are a mix of growth and value companies, and neither style overwhelms the other.

The growth and value styles go in and out of favor. One may dominate for a few years, and then the other will take the lead. Rather than bet which one is about to heat up, it's good to have investments reflecting both styles. A blend-oriented fund can also do the job.

STYLE POINTS

Below is a chart of how growth and value stocks did in the 1996 to 2005 period. The numbers, compiled by Standard & Poor's and Barra Investments, represent the annual percentage return for stocks in the S&P 500 that are classified as growth or value:

	1996	1997	1998	1999	2000	2001	2002	2003	2004	2005
S&P 500	22.96	33.36	28.58	21.04	−9.11	−11.89	−22.10	28.68	10.88	4.91
S&P MidCap 400	19.06	32.00	18.91	14.54	17.44	−.64	−14.43	35.34	16.35	12.47
Russell 2000	16.49	22.36	−2.55	21.26	−3.02	2.49	−20.48	47.25	18.33	4.55

The chart shows how the growth style captured the hearts and wallets of investors during the late '90s tech boom. Look at the spreads in 1998 and 1999. However, the correction hit the growth sector harder, with a 28 percent spread in the year 2000. Value also outperformed during the three years of the recovery in 2003 to 2005.

While this shows how volatile stock investing can be, it also illustrates that investors can reduce the turmoil by constructing a well-diversified mix of investments.

CHART YOUR COURSE

We have described how U.S. stocks and stock mutual funds have varying sizes and styles. Morningstar, an investment research firm in Chicago, is famous for its style box approach to categorizing mutual funds. Every stock mutual fund fits into one of nine boxes that show the broad characteristics of the fund.

	Value	Blend	Growth
Large	Large Value	Large Blend	Large Growth
Midcap	Midcap Value	Midcap Blend	Midcap Growth
Small	Small Value	Small Blend	Small Growth

Morningstar® Style Box

Referring to the style box illustration, you can draw some conclusions about the funds you own, or are researching. For example, large-value stock funds, in the upper left corner of the box, are the most conservative stock funds. They have stocks of large companies, which are less volatile than small company stocks, and they have a value orientation, which is less aggressive than a growth style. Conversely, the most aggressive funds reside in the small-growth box in the lower right-hand corner.

As you review your stock investments, it's a good idea to draw a box, like the one on page 131, and lay out where all the stock funds you own belong. You can usually determine a fund's category by looking at its prospectus, a legally required document that spells out the fund's investment objective and other information. If you are not sure how to classify your fund, you can look it up on Morningstar's website at www.morningstar.com.

Once you have determined which boxes all of your current fund holdings go into, enter in the appropriate boxes the dollar value of each fund that you own. Add up the total of all your stock fund holdings, and then determine what percentage of your investments resides in each box. That gives you an X-ray of your portfolio, a visual reference of your stock investments. If all of your stock funds are in just one or two boxes, you should be better diversified. If the overwhelming dollar amount of your stock investments falls within one box, you are taking on too much risk, and missing other opportunities.

Profits and Prices

Mutual funds undergo a multipart screening process to receive a growth, value, or blend label. One critical test is the price/earnings ratio, or P/E ratio. The P/E ratio tells you how much an investor must pay in stock price for every $1 worth of company earnings. For example, if a company makes an annual profit of $100 million, and if it has issued 100 million shares of stock, it makes a profit of $1 per share. If the stock costs $22 per share, it has a P/E of 22. ($22 divided by $1 equals 22.)

If another company makes $50 million and has 100 million shares outstanding, its profits are 50 cents per share. If the stock sells for $5 per share, the P/E ratio is 10. ($5 divided by $.50 equals 10.)

The reason some investors are willing to pay $22 for $1 in earnings, while others pay only $10 for $1 in earnings, is that the company with the $22 stock is growing more rapidly, and may soon have considerably higher profits. The market expects the stock with a P/E of 10 to plod along more slowly.

If the average P/E ratio of all stocks is, say, 17, then a stock with a P/E of 22 is a growth stock. The stock with a P/E of 10 is a value stock. Mutual funds get their style classification based on several factors, including the average P/E ratio of all stocks in the fund.

MAKING YOUR PICKS

You don't need an investment in each of the nine style boxes, but you should have at least one investment in each of the three size categories. Most stock investors have the largest share of their stock holdings in large caps. That makes sense, since the market capitalization of the S&P 500 totals about 80 percent of the total value of all publicly traded U.S. stocks. However, the small and mid cap sectors play an important role in a well-balanced portfolio. When it comes to style, decide how much risk you want to take. If you want to be aggressive, favor the growth style. If you want to be more cautious, lean toward value funds. For a moderate course, take a blend approach.

When selecting a new fund, first see if a category is missing from your current investments. If you need to fill a hole in your portfolio, start researching funds in that missing category. If it's a 401(k) investment, you may only have one option in the area.

If you have multiple choices, look for a fund that has performed well against similar type investments over three- and five-year periods. A fund that was hot in the past year may have done well by taking risky bets, and could be poised for a fall as the market rotates to new hot sectors. Look for longer periods of above average performance. Detailed information on nearly all funds is available at www.morningstar.com. They have premium services that you can purchase, but plenty of fund information is available at no charge.

There is no ideal mix of investments. The same principles of asset allocation and diversification pertain to all investors, but applying those principles can vary widely between individual investors. In the next chapter, we will suggest some model portfolios, but we still have several major investment categories to explore.

GOING GLOBAL IN A FLAT WORLD

In 2005, *New York Times* columnist Thomas L. Friedman wrote a book called *The World Is Flat.* Friedman argued that many of the advantages long held by the world's leading economies are flattening out, and becoming available all over the world. Factors such as computers, software, communications technology, and skilled workers are nearly as abundant in Bangalore as in Boston. Only the workers in Bangalore don't expect to be paid as much. While this global competition is hurting some Americans, the least we can do is try to make back some of our money by investing overseas.

Investors can choose from among hundreds of international stock funds. Many of these funds invest in large established companies in advanced economies such as Europe, Japan, and Australia. Some funds, called emerging market funds, invest in developing nations such as Brazil, South Korea, and Russia. Both of these categories expose you to companies outside the United States that are growing and making profits, often because America is their best customer.

International investing also increases diversification, which helps to manage risk. International stocks tend to be more volatile than U.S. stocks, and emerging market stocks are extremely volatile. Of course, that volatility applies to gains as well as losses. For instance, the DWS Emerging Markets Equity Fund dropped a gut-wrenching 29.93 percent in 2000, but rocketed back up 56.59 percent in 2003. The most widely used international stock index, the Morgan Stanley Europe, Australia, and Far East (EAFE) Index, topped all major U.S. indexes in 5 of the 20 years between 1986 and 2005. Its best year during that time was a stunning 69.46 percent gain in 1986. Its worst year was 1990, when the EAFE index lost 23.45 percent.

Though international funds tend to be more volatile than U.S. stock funds, studies show that adding some international salsa to your portfolio can increase both performance *and* stability. It is counterintuitive that adding something more volatile to the mix reduces overall volatility, but that's how the magic of diversification works.

Get a Load of This

Investors pay for mutual funds in two primary ways: up-front sales charges, or "loads," and management fees charged for the costs of operating the fund. Loads are sales charges paid to financial advisors for providing advice and selling a fund to a client. Investors have a legal right to know what those charges are. If you make your own fund selections, you should get "no-load" funds, which have no up-front sales charges.

The "expense ratio" is what the fund company charges to manage the fund. That pays for research and staff, for marketing, printing, legal work, and the many other costs of running a fund. The expense ratio is the percentage of the fund's total assets charged for fund management. According to Morningstar, in 2005 the typical retail investor paid 0.93 percent in expenses for a U.S. stock fund and 1.10 percent for an international stock fund. Bond funds averaged 0.85 percent. Many stock index funds, which are not actively managed, charge in the area of 0.20 percent, or 20 cents for every $100 invested.

KEY POINTS OF STOCK INVESTING

- Stock mutual funds offer diversification and professional management.
- Stock funds have many different investment objectives.
- Determine if a fund invests in large, small, or midsize companies.

- More aggressive funds have a growth orientation; value funds are less aggressive.
- Having a diverse mix of investments reduces volatility.
- International stock funds can improve performance *and* lower volatility.
- Consider the "expense ratio" in selecting a fund.

GETTING A FIX ON FIXED-INCOME INVESTMENTS

As a bondholder, you are lending money to companies or government entities. They pay interest on the loan and then repay the principal when the bond matures. Because bonds pay a fixed rate of interest, they are called fixed-income investments.

Bonds mature over different lengths of time. If you buy a one-year U.S. Treasury bill, Uncle Sam pays you back in a year. An intermediate-term bond matures in 3 to 10 years. A long-term bond could run for up to 30 years. Generally, the longer the term of the bond, the higher the interest rate it pays. Bond prices go up and down as interest rates change, and longer maturity bonds have more pronounced price swings.

Bonds also have different degrees of risk. The marketplace considers U.S. government securities as the safest of bonds. Despite the size of our budget deficits and national debt, investors feel the U.S. government will somehow always make good on its bonds. Corporate bonds carry a wide range of risk, from rock solid debt issued by blue chip companies, to so-called "junk bonds" issued by companies whose financial condition is less than pristine. Investors willing to purchase junk bonds, called "high-yield bonds" in polite company, receive a higher interest rate in return for assuming the higher risk. If a company has financial troubles it may default on its bonds, and bondholders can lose out. Rating agencies scrutinize bond issuers and rank them by financial strength and stability.

Bond mutual funds buy a portfolio of dozens or hundreds of bonds. As the fund collects interest payments, it passes them along each month to fund holders. Mutual funds are constantly buying new bonds as money comes into the fund, or shareholders reinvest their monthly interest payments. The share price of a bond mutual fund goes up and down on a daily basis as interest rates in the economy fluctuate.

Why Bond Prices Go Up or Down as Interest Rates Change

Bonds are usually a more stable investment than stocks, but when interest rates rise, bonds can also have you reaching for the Maalox. If you purchased a $1,000 bond with a six percent interest rate, you would receive $60 a year in interest. If rates later rose so that new bonds were yielding seven percent, or $70 a year, the price of your bond would go down. No one would pay $1,000 for your six percent bond when they could purchase a new bond yielding seven percent. The price of your six percent bond would drop until it reached a yield equivalent to seven percent bonds. Conversely, if rates dropped to five percent, your six percent bond would go up in value.

A bond mutual fund holds dozens or hundreds of bonds. As interest rates change every day, the value of bonds in the fund goes up and down, and so does the share price of the fund. The longer the maturity of a bond, the more its price will change. If rates rise, someone holding a 15-year long-term bond would see a bigger price drop than the holder of a 3-year bond. That's because the holder of the long-term bond must wait much longer to get his principal back, before he can reinvest at a more favorable rate. That makes his 15-year bond less attractive, so it takes a bigger hit.

BONDS HAVE STYLE, TOO

Just as stock funds have many different investment styles, a wide variety of bond funds are available. Some invest in short-term bonds, others concentrate on bonds with intermediate maturities, while others invest in long-term securities. Many bond funds focus on particular segments of the market, such as the following:

- U.S. government bonds
- Government agency bonds
- Municipal bonds
- Corporate bonds
- High-yield bonds
- International bonds

While stock funds are differentiated by the size of stocks in the fund and the growth and value styles, bond funds are categorized by credit quality and maturities. Credit quality means the financial strength of the company or government entity issuing the bond. Is it a high-risk bond, or a sure bet? Maturity is the length of the term of the bond: short, intermediate, long.

Here again, Morningstar has a style box that graphically displays a bond's basic characteristics:

Large	Large Value	Large Blend	Large Growth
Midcap	Midcap Value	Midcap Blend	Midcap Growth
Small	Small Value	Small Blend	Small Growth

Morningstar® Style Box

Looking at the upper left corner of the chart, a short-term bond from a high quality issuer is the safest investment. A one-year U.S. Treasury bill is an example from this category. It is short term, so it is not volatile, and it is from the safest possible source, the U.S. government.

The opposite corner, lower right, is the most volatile bond category, a long-term, low quality bond. This might be a "high-yield" bond with a 20-year maturity. The long term of the bond makes it volatile, and the weak financial status of the company issuing the bond makes it far riskier than U.S. government debt. But, in return for accepting that risk, the bondholder gets a higher rate of interest than a government bond would pay.

Bond fund holders get their total return from two sources: interest payments, and the capital gain or loss resulting from changes in interest rates. Though bond prices are generally more stable than stock prices, the return from bond funds can vary considerably over the years. The Lehman Brothers Aggregate Bond Index represents a composite of the overall bond market. In the 20 years between 1986 and 2005, the best year for bonds was 1991 when the index gained 16 percent. The worst year was 1994, when interest rates rose, and the index lost 2.92 percent. Over that 20-year period, the bond index beat all the major stock indexes two times.

KEY POINTS OF BOND FUND INVESTING

- When you own a bond fund, you are lending money to bond issuers.
- Bonds pay interest until the principal is repaid at maturity.
- Bonds have different maturities and credit quality.
- Long-term bonds are more volatile than short-term bonds.
- Bond prices move in the opposite direction to changes in interest rates.
- Higher-risk bonds pay higher rates of interest.
- Bonds can reduce portfolio volatility.

Bonds to the Rescue

Since bonds yield monthly interest income, you can either reinvest that money, or take it in cash once you are living off your investments. Because bonds are less volatile than stocks, and often move in a different direction than stocks, they cut down on portfolio volatility. Take the example of a Boomer with half her money invested in stocks and half in bonds. Let's assume stocks had a bad year and go down 10 percent, while bond investments go up 5 percent. Half of her investments would be subject to a 10 percent loss, resulting in a 5 percent drop in her portfolio. And half of her investments would be up 5 percent, lifting her portfolio by 2.5 percent. Her net loss would be just 2.5 percent in a year when there would be loud wailing about a terrible market. With such a modest loss, it's easy to keep your composure while others are hitting the panic button.

CASH ON THE BARREL

We will look at one final asset class and then get down to business in constructing some model portfolios. That final category is "cash." Cash investments are safe; they don't fluctuate in value, but they don't return much, either. Along with stocks and bonds, cash is one of the "Big 3" asset classes, but if you are investing for long-term growth, cash should play only a small role.

The most popular cash investments are the simple bank savings account and the certificate of deposit. These accounts pay interest, but usually not much above the rate of inflation.

Cash accounts are useful for holding money you many need on short notice, such as an emergency reserve fund. They can also be a temporary parking place for money you intend to invest elsewhere.

Money market mutual funds usually pay higher interest than bank accounts, and many have the convenience of check writing. Most investment portfolios have a money market account to receive dividends or interest payments, or as a safe place to hold money during an uncertain market. However, the purpose of the cash account is all about safety and preserving capital, not about growth.

CASH IN RETIREMENT PLANS

Most 401(k) plans have several cash options, and some are more attractive than the lowly savings account. These are some of the typical cash options available in workplace retirement plans:

- **Money market mutual fund:** These funds make short-term loans to high quality government and corporate borrowers. The funds maintain a share price of $1, and pay interest monthly. They are not FDIC insured.
- **Stable Value Funds:** High quality bonds and interest-bearing contracts, purchased from banks, insurance companies, or mutual funds that guarantee the value of principal and all accumulated interest. Available in about two-thirds of 401(k) plans. Usually pays higher interest than money market fund.
- **Guaranteed Investment Contracts (GICs):** These are issued by insurance companies that pay a fixed rate of interest for a fixed period. GICs can also be a blend of several investment contracts that pay a variable rate of interest, generally higher than a money market account. Despite the name, they are not guaranteed by any government agency.

LONG-TERM RETURNS

Following are the average annual returns, over the past 81 years of the major investment classes we've been discussing:

Large U.S. stocks:	10.4%
Small U.S. stocks:	12.7%

| Intermediate government bonds: | 5.3% |
| U.S. Treasury Bills (cash): | 3.7% |

Source: Stocks, Bonds, Bills, and Inflation 2007 Yearbook © Morningstar

Investment returns are eroded by inflation, which has averaged 3 percent over the past 81 years. After inflation and taxes, much of the gain of cash and bond investments is lost.

In putting together a portfolio, match your investments to your time horizon. If your savings goal is many years away, you can take on more risk with stock funds. If the market goes down, you have many years in which to make back your losses.

If you have a short-term goal, such as buying a house in a year or two, use a money market account and short-term bonds to reduce the risk of a big loss just before you need the money.

In the next chapter, we will take these investing fundamentals to construct several model portfolios, and look at how you can take full advantage of a 401(k) or similar workplace retirement plan.

9

MAKING THE MOST OF
YOUR 401(K)

Once upon a time there was a wonderful thing called a "defined benefit plan." Don't let the nerdy name fool you. It was the Ferrari of retirement schemes, allowing millions of Americans to bask in the sunshine in their golden years. The employer was totally responsible for setting aside and investing money for worker pensions. All the employees had to do was to show up for work, and put in their time. At retirement, they would collect a monthly check for the rest of their lives. If the stock market crashed, it was not the workers' problem. The boss just had to fork over more cash to the pension fund to make sure the checks went out like clockwork every month.

OK, so there still is such a thing as a "defined benefit plan," but it's right there next to the Siberian tiger on the endangered species list. The old style pension plan is loaded with costs and risk, so companies are dumping them in favor of the low budget alternative, the "defined contribution plan." The astute reader may notice that the operative word changed from "benefit" to "contribution."

The 401(k) is the king of defined contribution plans. Others in the realm include the 403(b) for many nonprofit workers and the

457 for some government employees. The numbers refer to sections of the Internal Revenue Code. The people who named these things were not marketing geniuses, just government bureaucrats. Wouldn't "The Dreammaker" have been a hotter title?

While traditional plans put all of the risk and burden of funding pensions onto employers, the 401(k) is the opposite. All of the risk and most of the burden falls upon the worker. Many companies match employee contributions up to a certain limit, but make no mistake: The heavy lifting in this deal is being done by Joe Employee. If there is not enough in the account when Joe wants to retire, that's his problem. If he didn't save enough or invest properly, too bad; Joe may just have to keep working into his seventies.

Despite that drawback, the 401(k) offers many advantages to employees. Most small businesses never provided a traditional pension. It was too costly. But many smaller employers can offer a 401(k), so that has extended pension opportunities to more workers.

The old-style pension generously rewarded lifetime service to a company, while skimping on benefits for short-term workers. But people change jobs more frequently these days, and the 401(k) is a portable pension, more suited to higher job turnover.

The 401(k) contains both risks and opportunities for U.S. workers. But the time to debate the merits of being a nation of amateur pension fund managers is behind us. It's a done deal. By applying the basic principles of investing covered in the previous chapter, and by learning the fundamentals of your 401(k) plan, you *can* be your own pension fund manager, even if you won't have Warren Buffett looking over your shoulder.

RULES OF THE ROAD

Like it or not, the 401(k) has become the most essential pieces of gear in the Boomer Retirement Survival Kit. If you handle this baby right, you can actually save a small fortune. This chapter is devoted to helping you make the right moves while avoiding the pitfalls.

Since nobody likes to read the fine print, we'll start with the Quick Start Guide to the 401(k). If you know this stuff already, consider the following a warm-up exercise:

- You decide what percentage or dollar amount of your pay you want to contribute to your 401(k).
- Whatever you contribute goes into your account tax-deferred, meaning income taxes are not taken out.
- Many employers match at least some of your contribution, but are not required to do so.
- You choose how the money should be invested from a number of different options.
- It is your job to monitor the account and make adjustments as necessary.
- Most plans allow you to borrow from your account.
- When you leave your job or retire, you have several options available to keep the money in a tax-deferred account.
- If you take money out of the account before age 59 and a half, you must pay income taxes, and in most cases, a 10 percent penalty for making a premature withdrawal.
- When you withdraw funds after age 59 and a half, you just pay the income tax due.
- Once retired, you must begin withdrawing money by age 70 and a half.

GIVE YOURSELF A (TAX) BREAK

Step one is deciding how much to contribute to your account. The first commandment of 401(k) contributions is to save at least as much as the company will match. If the company puts in 50 cents for every dollar you save, up to six percent of pay, then contribute six percent, even if you have to rent out your son's bedroom while he's away at college. By saving six percent of your pay, your employer kicks in an extra three percent. This is like getting an immediate 50 percent return on your investment. As Martha Stewart would say, "It's a good thing." If you contribute less, you are giving up free money.

For those who can afford it, tax rules in 2007 allow workers 50 and over to dump up to $20,500 a year into a 401(k). The limit for younger folks is $15,500. Congress gave fifty-plus workers a "catch-up" provision, and heaven knows most of us have some catching up to do. But some employer plans limit the percentage of pay you can contribute, so if your income is too low you may hit the percentage ceiling before you reach the maximum contribution limit.

The federal government gives you a big tax incentive to invest in your 401(k). In return for being an upstanding citizen and stashing away some loot for retirement, you get to postpone paying taxes on the income.

For example, by saving $5,000 a year in a 401(k), a worker might cut his tax bill by $1,000. The tax is eventually paid when money is taken out of the account during retirement, but that may be decades away. In the meantime, the money is in his account growing and compounding. It's like getting a bill for $1,000 that's not due for 10 or 20 years, or more. If only all our bills came that way.

The 401(k) offers another tax deferral bonus. Earnings in the account also evade the grasp of the IRS. If you owned a mutual fund outside of a retirement account, you would have to pay taxes on gains every year. But inside the comfy confines of your 401(k), all those gains stay right in there, continuing to compound and grow. Over a long period, the turbo-charge of tax deferral could boost your savings by thousands of dollars.

GET YOUR CHEESEBURGER IN PARADISE

Deciding how much to save is the easy part. Now it gets a little trickier. How are you going to invest the money? Here is where you do that Warren Buffett imitation. We know you'd rather listen to Jimmy Buffett, but if that's all you do, you'll never get your cheeseburger in paradise.

If ever there was a "one size does not fit all" situation, investing is it. A twenty-five-year-old investor has a completely different set of investment circumstances than a fifty-five-year-old. The twenty-five-year-old can afford to invest aggressively because when (not if) the stock market tanks, she has many years in which to recover her losses. The fifty-five-year-old has a much shorter time frame to bounce back from a bear market, and so midlife investors should generally take a more conservative approach.

That does not mean putting all your money in CDs or burying it in the backyard. Unless you are really loaded and can happily live off the interest on a few million bucks in government bonds, you need to establish a combination of investments that will meet your goals. Even at 55, you have a long investment time horizon and so stocks, or stock mutual funds, have an important role.

Choosing an asset allocation is a personal decision. Most Boomers in their forties will make a different choice than those in their sixties, but some experienced sixty-year-old investors may be more aggressive than people in their forties who can't stomach market volatility. A portfolio that is heavy in stocks can go down dramatically in any given year. If you can't stand the heat, don't go into the kitchen. We all have to understand our own tolerance for risk. Many people sell their stock funds when the market gets choppy, and then miss the rebound when stocks come roaring back a year or two later. That's called buying high and selling low. It's a recipe for Hamburger Helper, not a cheeseburger in paradise.

WHAT COLOR IS YOUR PORTFOLIO?

For too many 401(k) participants, the names of all the funds in their plans are a confusing blur. It's like the wine novice who picks a bottle based on an appealing label, hoping things will work out at dinner that night. Too much is riding on your 401(k) for guesswork. You need to be more of a connoisseur.

You start with the basic asset allocation question: What percentage of your investments do you want in stocks, bonds, or cash? If it helps, make a pie chart to visualize your allocation. No one can prescribe a blanket asset allocation for a particular age group. Your own decision will depend on how long you have until retirement, your tolerance for risk, how much savings you have accumulated, and whether you have a pension or other assets available at retirement. Whether you expect to receive a large inheritance or intend to leave an estate can also affect your investment plan.

While one size does not fit all, we want to suggest a starting point for your own asset allocation deliberations. Below are a series of hypothetical investment plans for Boomers with different retirement target dates. You must make your own choices, but these are portfolios that a financial planner might recommend to a client who understands market volatility and the principles of risk and reward.

RETIRE IN 5 YEARS

60 percent stocks
35 percent bonds
5 percent cash

Stocks

40 percent S&P 500 Index fund
5 percent mid cap growth fund
5 percent small cap value fund
10 percent international fund

Bonds

20 percent intermediate bond fund
10 percent short-term bond fund
5 percent high-yield bond fund

Cash

5 percent stable value fund

Analysis

A Boomer with five years before retirement needs portfolio growth, but cannot take big risks so close to a drop-off in employment income. This 60-35-5 portfolio is designed for growth with stability. The S&P 500 Index fund, a large cap blend fund, is the core holding. A small holding in the mid cap area is invested for growth. The more aggressive small cap fund has a less volatile value orientation. The international fund provides both diversification and a growth opportunity.

Rising interest rates are a major concern for bondholders, so it's good to invest in bond funds with lower volatility. The largest bond holding is an intermediate bond fund. If interest rates rise, the intermediate fund will be less volatile than a long-term bond fund. The short-term bond fund reduces risk further in a rising rate environment. The high-yield fund offers a little extra kick in interest income, while further diversifying the bond holdings.

In the cash category, a stable value fund generally outperforms a money market account with a high degree of safety.

RETIRE IN 10 YEARS

65 percent stocks
35 percent bonds

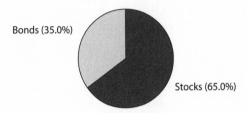

Bonds (35.0%)

Stocks (65.0%)

Stocks

40 percent S&P 500 Index fund
5 percent mid cap growth fund
5 percent small cap growth fund
10 percent international fund
5 percent emerging markets fund

Bonds

20 percent intermediate bond fund
10 percent short-term bond fund
5 percent high-yield bond fund

Analysis

With 10 years to go until retirement, an investor has time to ride out and recover from most bear markets, based on historical returns. That allows for a little more aggressive approach, which is likely to be rewarded with a higher return. The 65-35 portfolio not only has a slightly more aggressive asset allocation, but has more of a growth orientation. The mid cap fund has a growth style, and we have added a small position in an emerging markets stock fund.

The bond holdings are the same as the five-year portfolio. The cash account has been eliminated.

RETIRE IN 15 YEARS

72 percent stocks
28 percent bonds

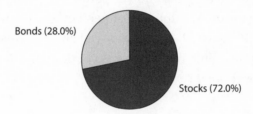

Bonds (28.0%)

Stocks (72.0%)

Stocks

42 percent S&P 500 Index fund
7 percent mid cap growth fund
7 percent small cap growth fund
11 percent international fund
5 percent emerging markets fund

Bonds

15 percent intermediate bond fund
8 percent short-term bond fund
5 percent high-yield bond fund

Analysis

Fifteen years out from retirement, a Boomer can go for a little more gusto with an aggressive portfolio. Stocks make up almost three-quarters of the account. The S&P 500 Index fund remains the core holding, but 30 percent of the portfolio is invested more aggressively in the mid and small cap areas, and the international and emerging markets funds.

The bond holdings are relatively low risk, and will help to offset losses in a stock downturn. For example, if the stock market dropped by 10 percent in a given year, that would be a 7.2 percent loss from stocks in the portfolio (72 percent of the 10 percent drop). If, in that year, the bond market returned 6 percent, that would provide a 1.8 percent gain to the portfolio (28 percent of the 6 percent gain). The total loss for the portfolio is 5.4 percent, disappointing but not devastating. Of course, losses can exceed this example, but with a 15-year investment time frame, the risks of this portfolio are likely to be rewarded with solid returns.

RETIRE IN 20 YEARS

80 percent stocks
20 percent bonds

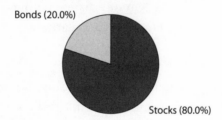

Bonds (20.0%)

Stocks (80.0%)

Stocks

45 percent S&P 500 Index fund
9 percent mid cap growth fund
9 percent small cap growth fund
12 percent international fund
5 percent emerging markets fund

Bonds

> 10 percent intermediate bond fund
> 5 percent short-term bond fund
> 5 percent high-yield bond fund

Analysis

This is an aggressive asset allocation, with four out of five dollars invested in stocks. Large U.S. stocks with a blend style are the biggest holding through the S&P 500 Index fund. The more volatile mid and small cap funds, along with the international and emerging markets funds, make up more than one-third of the portfolio. This mix has the potential to be volatile. That means losses in years when the markets are tanking. But it is well diversified, and could produce excellent returns in the good years.

The 20 percent of the account invested in bonds helps to offset the risk of the high stock concentration. This is not a portfolio for Boomers with a low risk tolerance, but it could work for the investor who is willing to ride out volatility in return for solid long-term results.

MODEL PORTFOLIOS SUMMARY

Each suggested portfolio contains seven or eight mutual funds that focus on different parts of the investing universe. They provide an asset allocation that gets more conservative the closer a Boomer is to retirement. Boomers with many years until retirement should understand that being too conservative also carries risks. A long-term portfolio that skimps on stocks may avoid the occasional bear market mauling. But it may also grow so slowly that it fails to generate the savings you'll need for retirement security.

You can use one of these portfolio models or create your own. Once you determine the specifications of the portfolio you want, you have to identify the funds in your menu of 401(k) options that match your desired mix of investments. The printed materials provided by your 401(k) plan describe the investment theme of each fund in the plan, i.e., large value stocks, short-term bonds, etc. If those explanations are unclear, you can also look up the style and performance history of virtually any mutual fund at www.morningstar.com.

If you are just starting a 401(k) plan, following these guidelines will help you to establish your investment mix. If you are already in a plan, consider these models to see if your portfolio needs a tune-up, or a major overhaul. If you decide to make changes to an existing plan, devise a strategy for reaching your target by moving money between funds, and/or changing the allocation of future contributions.

HITTING THE TARGET

An alternative to assembling your own portfolio is the growing use of target-date retirement funds, sometimes referred to as "life cycle" funds. These are ready-made portfolios geared to investors with specific retirement dates. For example, portfolios are tailored for retirement in 2010, 2015, 2020, 2025, and so on. You pick the fund that matches your intended retirement date, and the fund manager picks an assortment of stock and bond funds that match your goal. The basic stock, bond, and cash allocations are based on the investment time horizon, with each category holding funds from a variety of investment styles. As the years pass, the portfolio is adjusted to meet your shorter time horizon. You get ongoing asset allocation and diversification with one investment.

Some critics contend that no mutual fund company has winning funds in all investment categories, so you may have some poorly performing funds in a target-date plan. But given all the advantages of these prefab portfolios, they are a choice worth considering.

LOOK AT THE BIG PICTURE

In choosing your portfolio, do not look at your 401(k) plan in isolation. You may have several retirement accounts, including an IRA, a 401(k) at a past employer, a rollover IRA, or an SEP account, if you have been self-employed. If you are married or have a partner, he or she may also have a patchwork of retirement accounts. Since all of these accounts have the same purpose—funding your retirement—they should be coordinated to work together.

Total up all your retirement investments, draw a pie chart, and write down your overall asset allocation between stocks, bonds, and cash. Then, go back to the Morningstar style box (described in the previous chapter) and list ALL of your retirement investments on a single chart. Make sure your diversification between market caps and growth/value styles is what it should be. If the big picture is out of balance, you can move funds around in other accounts, or adjust your 401(k) to get your overall portfolio on track.

EMOTIONS ARE HAZARDOUS TO YOUR PORTFOLIO

Once you have decided on your asset allocation and mix of investments, stick to your game plan. Financial markets go through all kinds of gyrations. Every night you can hear analysts explain why stocks went up or down that day. If you get caught up in all that market "noise" you may be tempted to make impulsive investment choices, rather than staying true to the plan you deliberately set up.

Acting on emotion almost always works against an investor. Human nature dictates that we want to sell stocks when the market drops, and buy when stocks are doing great. In fact, doing the opposite is better. If you buy when the market is down you get shares at a discount; buying into a hot market means you pay top dollar.

When the inevitable bear market strikes, stocks usually regain all of their losses within five years. That can feel like a long time. But if you keep investing during that low period you accumulate new shares at favorable prices. Then, when the market comes back and surpasses its old high point, your pre-bear investment is recouped, and the new shares you bought along the way make solid gains. Be patient. Let the market do the work for you.

MAINTAIN YOUR BALANCE

Every so often you need to rebalance your 401(k) investments. If you set up an asset allocation with 70 percent in stocks and 30 percent in bonds, movement in the markets will change that ratio over time. If stocks do well for a year or two, you could end up with an allocation of 80 percent stocks and 20 percent bonds. That's a more aggressive portfolio, and if you don't do something about it, you will lose control over your asset allocation, which is the major driver of portfolio risk.

Keep Beneficiaries Up to Date

When you sign up for a 401(k), you are asked to name a beneficiary who will receive your 401(k) savings if you die. Keep your beneficiary information up to date with all your financial accounts. If you get divorced or married, or experience any major life-changing event, think about whether it affects your 401(k), your will, insurance policies, deed to your home, and savings and investment accounts. More than one person has died and mistakenly left assets to a former spouse.

To rebalance your account, transfer money out of the investments that exceed your desired allocation, and into the categories that have become under weighted. You may also want to change your contributions until the portfolio is back in balance. You don't have to do this too often; a few percentage points change is not a concern. But once a year you should check to see that your portfolio matches the asset allocation you desire.

BORROWING TROUBLE

Most 401(k) plans allow participants to borrow from their account. For Boomers closing in on retirement, this is generally not a good idea. A loan reduces the amount of money in the account that grows tax-deferred. This can undermine investment results. The loan amount, plus interest, has to be paid back by the employee through payroll deduction. The interest rate is generally one or two percent above the prime rate. That may be less than the money would earn if it remained in the account. The account balance can also take a hit if the employee lowers 401(k) contributions while paying off the loan.

Generally, loans must be paid back within five years. If you are laid off or leave your job during that time, you must pay back the entire balance, or that amount will be treated as an early distribution. Early distributions are subject to income tax plus a 10 percent penalty for those under age 59 and a half. If you are laid off, the last thing you want to do is fork over several thousand dollars to pay off a loan. Loan repayments are made with after-tax dollars. When the funds are finally withdrawn during retirement, they are subject to income taxes again.

Boomers, especially those over 50, should only consider a 401(k) loan as a last resort. At this stage of our lives, we need to focus on preparing for the future. The 401(k) is a centerpiece of that planning. Anything that undermines the healthy growth of a 401(k) account should be avoided.

ROLLOVER BEETHOVEN

When you leave a job you have to decide what to do with your 401(k) account. You have several options. Often, you can keep your 401(k) funds in your old employer's plan. You may be able to transfer the account into the 401(k) of a new employer, if you are changing jobs. The worst option is to treat the money like a windfall and take it in cash. That's an early withdrawal, subject to income tax and a 10 percent penalty for those under age 59 and a half. More important, it blows a big hole in a worker's retirement nest egg.

The best option may be to transfer the funds into an IRA rollover account. It's like an IRA except that it is funded by money from your 401(k) rather than an annual contribution. As an IRA, the money continues to grow tax-deferred, and you have a wide variety of investment choices. If you open the account with a large financial services company, you can choose from a full range of mutual funds, or a brokerage account that lets you trade individual stocks and bonds.

If you are leaving a job, set up the IRA rollover account before any money changes hands. Just apply to open the account and get an account number. Then, your old employer's 401(k) provider will give you the forms to fill out instructing them where to send the money. It's a routine transaction and should go off without a hitch.

Rollover Pitfall

If you want to set up an IRA rollover account, do not have 401(k) money sent to you with your name on the check. That will be recorded as an early withdrawal, and your employer will withhold 20 percent of your account balance to go toward taxes on the withdrawal. If you had $250,000 in the account, you'll only receive $200,000. You have 60 days from receipt of the check to deposit the money in an IRA rollover. You can get your $50,000 back when you file your taxes, but only if you deposit the full $250,000 in the IRA rollover. If you deposit just the $200,000 you received, the $50,000 shortfall will be judged as an early withdrawal, and you will have to pay taxes and possibly a 10 percent penalty on that amount. To avoid that, you would have to come up with $50,000 from another source to make the full $250,000 rollover payment within 60 days. There is a heavy-handed catch-22 aspect to all this, so just keep it simple, and set up the direct IRA rollover as described above.

10

RETIREMENT SAVINGS TOOLBOX

For most Boomers, the 401(k) or similar plan is the workhorse in our retirement saving stable, but not all employers offer a 401(k). Some people are self-employed; some have spouses who are not working. A few people can max out on their 401(k) and still be looking for more tax-advantaged ways to save. Fortunately, many other retirement savings vehicles are available. In this chapter, we will test-drive the most popular alternatives. We'll also look under the hood of a big Boomer decision: when to start collecting Social Security.

Many of these investment plans, such as IRAs, SEPs, and annuities, have complicated rules. Deciphering the fine print looks about as enticing as walking on a bed of hot coals. As a result, many people skip using these options, even though they are valuable implements in the retirement savings toolbox. We'll save you the migraine by breaking the plans down into their basic components, so you can see how they work and decide whether they are right for you.

INDIVIDUAL RETIREMENT ACCOUNTS

In 1985, when Congress put restrictions on taking tax deductions for investing in Individual Retirement Accounts (IRAs), many taxpayers stopped contributing. However, changes in the law since then have made IRAs more taxpayer friendly. If you gave up on the old IRA back in the '80s, you may want to revisit the rules to see if you can squeeze a tax break out of Uncle Sam while boosting your retirement savings. First, we'll look at traditional IRAs, and then we'll examine the Roth IRA.

Basic Purpose

An IRA allows taxpayers to put money into an investment account, which grows tax-deferred. The funds can stay in the account for years without any of the gains being taxed. Taxes are due when funds are taken out during retirement. Many taxpayers can deduct IRA contributions from current income.

Who Can Contribute to a Traditional IRA

- You must be under age 70 and a half at the end of the tax year.
- You, or your spouse if you file a joint return, must have employment income, such as wages, salaries, commissions, tips, bonuses, or net income from self employment. (Taxable alimony is income for IRA purposes. Compensation does not include rental income, interest and dividends, or pension or annuity income.)
- You can contribute to an IRA even if you participate in a retirement plan at work.

Where

You can set up an IRA at a bank or other financial institution, or with a mutual fund or life insurance company. You can also set up an IRA through your stockbroker.

When

Contributions can be made up to the tax filing deadline. If taxes are due April 15, you can contribute to an IRA that day and have it apply to the prior year. Be sure to indicate with your deposit the taxable year to which the contribution applies.

Contributions

Per person contribution limits have risen in recent years, and special "catch-up" provisions allow those age 50 and older to contribute even more.

For 2007:

- Regular IRA maximum contribution: $4,000
- Maximum contribution for age 50+: $5,000

For 2008:

- Regular IRA maximum contribution: $5,000
- Maximum contribution for age 50+: $6,000

Contributions cannot exceed employment earnings. In other words, you can't contribute more than you make.

Spousal Contribution

If one spouse has employment income and other does not, IRA contributions can be made for both. The same per person maximum applies, as long as household income exceeds the total of contributions. If the second spouse has income below the contribution limit, the spousal contribution can still be made for the maximum amount. If the spouse with earned income does not make an IRA contribution, the other spouse can still contribute.

Tax Deductions for 2007

- If neither you nor your spouse has a retirement plan at work, you can both deduct the full amount of your IRA contributions, *regardless of income.*
- If a married couple both have retirement plans at work they can fully deduct IRA contributions if modified adjusted gross income is below $83,000. The deduction is phased out for income between $83,000 and $103,000.
  Example: If income is $93,000, about half the IRA contribution is deductible. For income over $103,000, no deduction is available.
- If a single taxpayer or head of household has a retirement plan at work, income must be under $52,000 to a get a full deduction. A partial deduction is available if income is between $52,000 and $62,000. There is no deduction for income above $62,000.
- If your spouse is covered by a retirement plan at work, but you are not, you can fully deduct your IRA contribution if household income is below $156,000. The deduction is phased out for income between $156,000 and $166,000. If your income is $166,000 or more, you cannot take a deduction for IRA contributions. This also means that if one spouse works and has a retirement plan, and the second spouse does not have employment income, the spousal IRA is fully deductible if household

income is below $156,000, which is the case for about 95 percent of all U.S. households.

Nondeductible Contributions

Anyone who qualifies for an IRA can make a nondeductible contribution, regardless of income. The account is funded with after-tax dollars, but the earnings grow tax-deferred until taken out during retirement. The portion of a withdrawal that comes from after-tax contributions comes out tax-free. For those who qualify, contributing to a Roth IRA is preferable to making a nondeductible contribution to a traditional IRA. A full explanation of the Roth IRA is coming up.

All of the IRA income limits are based on what the IRS calls modified adjusted gross income, or MAGI. IRS Publication 590 has a worksheet to help you determine your MAGI. Go to the IRS website at www.irs.gov and search for Publication 590.

How to Invest

IRA money should be invested as part of an overall retirement savings plan. You want to maintain your desired asset allocation between stocks, bonds, and cash. IRA contributions should preserve that investment mix. If your allocation has gotten off track, use an IRA contribution to restore balance to your total portfolio.

Withdrawals

Once you put money into a traditional IRA, plan to keep it there until at least age 59 and a half. With a few exceptions, if you withdraw funds before 59 and a half, you will pay a 10 percent penalty on the withdrawal, in addition to whatever income taxes are due. The exceptions allowing for penalty-free withdrawals include qualified higher education expenses; qualified first home purchase (lifetime limit of $10,000); certain medical expenses; disability; expenses stemming from long-term unemployment; or taking annual withdrawals based on an IRS formula. Tread carefully here by consulting an accountant or studying IRS Publication 590.

You cannot borrow from your IRA or use it as security for a loan.

If you don't need to dip into your IRA, let it keep growing tax-deferred. But you must start taking distributions from your IRA by April 1 of the year following the year in which you reach age 70 and a half. Required minimum distributions are determined by an IRS formula based on life expectancies.

Example: You reach age 70 and a half on September 15, 2022. You must take the required minimum distribution by April 1, 2023. You would also need to receive another distribution for calendar year 2023 by December 31 of that year. At age 70, the IRS tables specify a distribution period of 27.4 years. If you have $200,000 in your IRA, the minimum distribution is $7,299 ($200,000/27.4). Failure to take the required minimum distribution results in tax penalties.

Transfers and Rollovers

If you are dissatisfied with the manager of your IRA, you can arrange a tax-free transfer directly from one fund manager to another. Investment companies are happy to provide the required paperwork. You can also withdraw funds from an IRA without tax or penalty, as long as you roll the money over into a new IRA within 60 days. This kind of rollover can only be done once per year. If you are ever in urgent need of cash that you *know* you can pay back within 60 days, you could dip into an IRA for that purpose, as long as you meet the rollover deadline.

ROTH IRA

Named after the late Republican Senator William Roth Jr. of Delaware, the Roth IRA took effect January 1, 1998, as part of the *Taxpayer Relief Act* of 1997.

Basic Purpose

A Roth IRA is a variation of the traditional IRA, but with a different twist on the tax benefits. With the traditional IRA, many taxpayers can take a tax deduction for their contributions and then pay taxes when they withdraw the funds. The Roth IRA is just the opposite. Contributions are made with after-tax dollars, but all the gains come out tax-free.

Who Can Contribute to a Roth IRA

- Unlike the traditional IRA, people over age 70 and a half can contribute to a Roth.
- As with a traditional IRA, you must have employment income to contribute to a Roth. However, if you make too much, contributions are prohibited. For 2007, those limits are the following:
    1. Joint tax filers with income below $156,000 can make Roth contributions up to the maximum permitted. For income between $156,000 and $166,000, a partial contribution can be made. If income exceeds $166,000, no contribution can be made.
    2. For single filers, full contributions are permitted for income below $99,000. Partial contributions can be made when income falls between $99,000 and $114,000. No contribution is allowed for income above $114,000.

Just to keep you off balance, the IRS has special rules for determining modified adjusted gross income (MAGI) for Roth IRAs. See IRS Publication 590 for details.

When and Where

Roth IRAs have the same application deadline as traditional IRAs and are available at virtually all of the banking and investment institutions that offer traditional IRAs.

Contributions

Contribution limits are the same for Roth IRAs as for the traditional IRAs. You can contribute to both a Roth and a traditional IRA in the same year, as long as total contributions do not exceed the annual IRA contribution limit. The same spousal contribution rules apply to a Roth IRA as to a traditional IRA. You can have a Roth even if you participate in a retirement plan at work.

The longer you intend to let funds grow in your retirement account, the more attractive a Roth IRA is. The instant gratification of an immediate tax deduction from an IRA contribution is a powerful inducement. But over 15 or 20 years, a Roth contribution could easily quadruple. Being able to withdraw those funds tax-free is more valuable than taking a tax deduction for the initial contribution.

If you expect to be in a much lower tax bracket in retirement than during your working years, deducting a traditional IRA contribution may be the better way to go. You would be able to deduct income while in a high tax bracket, and pay taxes while in the lower bracket.

Withdrawals

The amount you contribute to a Roth IRA can be withdrawn without tax or penalty at any time. You put in after-tax dollars, so they don't punish you for taking the money out. That's good flexibility to have, but you don't want to be too casual about raiding your retirement piggy bank.

The biggest attraction of the Roth IRA is that all of the earnings in the account can be tax-free. But you do have to jump over a couple of hurdles to win that prize:

1. You must not withdraw money until the account has been open for at least five years.
2. You take the money out after reaching age 59 and a half. (Tax-free withdrawals are also allowed if the Roth owner becomes disabled or uses the funds for the qualified purchase of a first home, or if the owner dies and leaves the IRA in an estate.)

If you withdraw the money before meeting the five-year requirement, taxes will be due on the earnings in the account. If you have not yet reached age 59 and a half, you may also have to pay that dreaded 10 percent penalty. Once you reach 59 and a half the penalty is waived, but tax is due if you break the five-year rule.

The clock starts ticking on the five years on January 1 of the calendar year when you make the first contribution. So even if you contribute in December, you get credit for that full year. In fact, a Roth contribution made before the April tax filing deadline gives you credit for the entire preceding year.

Unlike traditional IRAs, Roth IRAs do not have a required minimum distribution at age 70 and a half. That means the owner of a Roth IRA can let the account grow indefinitely without ever withdrawing the funds. Upon death, the account can be left to a spouse, or passed on tax-free in the estate, as long as the account had been open for at least five years. Similar to traditional IRAs, special distribution rules apply to Roth IRAs left in an estate. It's worth consulting a tax attorney or accountant to make the correct distributions.

Conversions

You can convert a traditional IRA to a Roth IRA. If you convert, you must pay the taxes due on the IRA in the year you make the conversion. Once that is done, all future growth in the account is tax-free, if you meet the withdrawal rules outlined above.

There is an income limit, however. You can only convert your regular IRA to a Roth IRA if your modified adjusted gross income is $100,000 or less, and if you are single or file jointly with your spouse.

The Tax Increase Prevention and Reconciliation Act, or TIPRA of 2005, will make conversions easier. The legislation gives investors the opportunity, starting in 2010, to convert traditional IRAs into Roth IRAs regardless of income. For conversions in 2010 individuals will be able to spread taxes due over a two-year period. Some higher income households that otherwise could not convert or even open a Roth are contributing to traditional IRAs through 2009, knowing they can convert to a Roth in 2010.

To make a conversion, contact the investment company that holds your IRA and ask for instructions. If you want to change companies, contact the firm where you would like to open the Roth IRA, and they will provide forms to enable a smooth transfer.

RETIREMENT PLANS FOR THE SELF-EMPLOYED

Retirement savings plans for the self-employed offer generous tax advantages. Whether you work for yourself full-time, or work for another employer but make a little money on the side, you can stash away a hefty percentage of self-employment income in a tax-deductible savings plan. We'll look at two options: the Simplified Employee Pension Plan, or SEP-IRA, and a newer alternative, the Self-Employed 401(k), or Solo 401(k), which offers a big boost in the amount that can be set aside for retirement.

SIMPLIFIED EMPLOYEE PENSION PLAN, OR SEP-IRA

The SEP-IRA is a retirement plan specifically designed for self-employed people and small-business owners. Our focus is on the self-employed individual. The SEP allows for tax-deductible contributions into an IRA. The SEP is potentially more attractive than a traditional IRA because the worker can make much larger tax-advantaged contributions into the account. As the name implies, these plans are simple to administer. There are no complicated forms to fill out, and no annual reports to file with the IRS.

Who Can Contribute to a SEP-IRA

You can contribute to a SEP if you meet the following criteria:

- You are a sole proprietor, in a partnership, or a business owner (of either an unincorporated or incorporated business, including Subchapter S corporations).
- You earn any self-employed income by providing a service, either full-time or part-time, even if you are already covered by a retirement plan at your full-time job.

When and Where

Many of the same financial institutions that offer traditional IRAs also have SEP-IRAs. You can set up a SEP as late as the due date (including extensions) of your income tax return for that year.

Contributions

- A SEP allows annual deductible contributions of up to 25 percent of compensation if your business is a corporation, or 20 percent of income if you are a sole proprietor. The maximum contribution for 2007 is $45,000.
- Contributions can be based on income up to $225,000 in 2007. A SEP-IRA contribution worksheet is available in IRS Publication 560. Most major mutual fund companies also have SEP-IRA calculators on their websites.
- Contributions are tax deductible, and grow tax-deferred.
- No annual contribution is required. Contribution percentage can vary each year, from 0 percent to 25 percent of compensation, up to the maximum dollar amount allowed.

Withdrawals

Distributions from a SEP-IRA are governed by the same rules as for a traditional IRA (see above).

SOLO 401(k)

The Economic Growth and Tax Relief Reconciliation Act of 2001 changed the law to allow self-employed workers to set up a 401(k) plan. The Self-Employed 401(k), or Solo 401(k), enables self-employed workers to save much more than they can with just a SEP. For Boomers who own a business and can afford to make the contributions, the Solo 401(k) is an excellent way to save aggressively for retirement.

Who Can Establish a Solo 401(k) Plan

A Solo 401(k) is available to self-employed individuals or business owners with no employees other than a spouse, including sole proprietors, partnerships, corporations, and S corporations. The Solo 401(k) is not appropriate for a business that has, or plans to add, any non-spouse employee who would be eligible to participate in the plan.

When and Where

The deadline to establish a Solo 401(k) is the end of the year (or fiscal year-end.) The deadline for depositing contributions into the plan is your tax filing deadline, generally April 15 plus extensions.

Not all financial services companies offer the Solo 401(k). Fidelity, T. Rowe Price, and American Century Investments are among those offering the plans. Check the websites of the financial institutions where you do business to see if they offer such a plan.

Contributions

- The Solo 401(k) offers double-barrel action when it comes to contributions. First, the business owner can make contributions up to the limit of a regular 401(k) plan, which is $15,500 in 2007. People age 50 and older can contribute an additional $5,000, for a total of $20,500.
- Second, if your business is a corporation, up to 25 percent of income can be contributed to a Solo 401(k). For sole proprietors, up to 20 percent of income can be contributed.

Example: A fifty-year-old sole proprietor with $100,000 of income can contribute up to the 401(k) limit of $20,500. He can also contribute another 20 percent of his income, or $20,000. Retirement savings contributions would total $40,500.

Using the same example, if the owner's business is a corporation, he could contribute the 401(k) maximum of $20,500, plus 25 percent of income, or another $25,000. Contributions would total $45,500.

Even though a Solo 401(k) enables this two-fisted approach to stashing away retirement savings, there is a limit to how much you can contribute. For 2007, the most that can be deposited into a Solo 401(k) is $45,000; the limit is $50,000 for people age 50 and older.

If you are a sole proprietor, you can deduct contributions from your personal income. If your business is incorporated, you can generally deduct contributions as a business expense.

Contributions are discretionary. You can load up your account in lucrative years, and skip a year when business is lean.

ANNUITIES

An annuity provides regular payments that last a lifetime. In this era of the 401(k) and rising health care costs, when individuals are taking on more financial risk, an annuity has the appeal of a rock-solid income stream that you can count on. The reliability of those payments is dependent on the financial strength of the insurance company that issues the annuity. You can research the financial strength ratings of insurance companies from A.M. Best at www.ambest.com.

Annuity Nuts and Bolts

An annuity is an insurance contract, but is available through many investment firms as well as insurance companies. The basic concept is simple: You give the company a sum of money and the company agrees to give you monthly payments for the rest of your life.

If someone buys a half-million-dollar annuity and drops dead in six months, the insurance company gets a windfall. If a sixty-five-year-old collects for 35 years, until age 100, the insurance company takes a hit. But that really gets to the heart of the annuity concept. Lasting to a ripe old age and outliving your money is a risk. The annuity shifts that risk from the individual to the insurance company. The company has so many accounts that the "early demisers" and the "longevity champs" offset each other, and the company can pretty well estimate its payment liabilities.

You make annuity contributions with after-tax dollars, but investment gains inside the annuity grow tax-deferred. When you eventually withdraw money, a portion of each payment is tax-free (from your principal), and a portion is taxable (from the annuity growth). Like an IRA, withdrawals before age 59 and a half are subject to a 10 percent penalty in addition to federal and state income taxes. Unlike an IRA, you do not have to start withdrawals from an annuity at age 70 and a half. There is no annual limit on how much you can contribute to an annuity.

Most financial advisors recommend maxing out on contributions to a 401(k) plan before considering purchase of an annuity. Contributions to a 401(k) are made with pretax dollars, so you get an immediate tax break, which annuities can't match.

Immediate or Deferred

You can purchase an immediate annuity and begin collecting monthly benefits right away. With a deferred annuity, your contributions are invested and the account grows until you are ready to start receiving payments.

Fixed or Variable

You can purchase either a fixed or a variable annuity. With a fixed annuity, your contributions grow at a fixed rate. When the time comes to start collecting from the annuity, you receive a fixed monthly payment that never changes. You can choose to have payments keep pace with inflation, but it means accepting a smaller monthly check in return. The fixed rate payment assigned to your account depends on prevailing interest rates when you start collecting. A study by benefits consultant Watson Wyatt Worldwide shows that in 1990, the monthly payment on a $100,000 annuity was $803. For those starting annuity payments in the low interest rate environment of 2006, the monthly check had shrunk to $584.

With variable annuities, your contributions go into a variety of investments, similar to stock and bond mutual funds, and the rate of return depends on investment results. When you start collecting, monthly payments are based on the size of the portfolio. Over time, payments will go up or down, depending on how the account performs. The appeal of the variable annuity is that a portfolio of stock funds may have better growth than a fixed annuity, if you hold the investment for a long period. You can have a variable annuity portfolio while building the account, and then switch to fixed payments when it's time to start collecting. Some annuities let you combine fixed and variable payouts to give you both an income floor and a chance for investment growth.

Payout Options

The most basic form of collecting from an annuity is a "single-life" option. It gives you the maximum monthly payment that lasts a lifetime, whether that lifetime is six months or 35 years. When you die, payments stop. No assets remain for a spouse or other heirs.

In return for accepting a smaller monthly payment, you can opt for a "joint and survivor" payout. This continues payments for the life of a surviving spouse.

Another option allows for a minimum number of payments, or "period certain," regardless of how long the annuity owner lives. For example, if the annuity calls for a minimum of 10 years of payments and the account holder dies 3 years into the contract, the heirs receive the balance in the account. In return for this protection, the monthly payment is lower than for the "single-life" option. The more protection you want, the lower the payments.

The "life annuity with cash refund" option gives you guaranteed income for life, and if the total income received is less than what you invested in the account, the difference is paid to your beneficiary.

Expenses

One drawback of some annuities is their expense. Like mutual funds, annuities charge for investment management services. In addition, annuities have an annual administrative fee, and a "mortality and expense risk charge," a phrase that is pure poetry to devotees of actuarial science. The mortality and expense risk charge covers two areas: the risk that some annuity owners will live longer than the company expects, and the cost of administering the contract if it exceeds projections. These are essentially insurance charges built in to the annuity fee structure. But it all adds up. Morningstar reports that the average variable annuity has an expense ratio of 2.38 percent of assets under management, more than twice as high as a typical stock mutual fund. On a $100,000 annuity, that's $2,380 in annual expenses. You can find many lower fee annuities, but you have to shop around.

In addition, many annuity contracts have up-front sales commissions and "surrender charges" if you take excess money out of the account during the first five to seven years. If you suddenly need access to a large lump sum and your money is tied up in an annuity, you may be hit with a costly surrender charge. When comparing annuities, check both the fee structures and the financial strength ratings of the companies you are researching.

Rollovers

A debate exists within the financial services industry about whether consumers should roll over IRA or 401(k) money into special qualified annuities. Retirement plans already have the tax deferral that annuities offer, and withdrawals from both types of accounts are taxed as ordinary income. But most annuities have higher annual expenses than retirement savings plans, and that cuts into investment returns.

The pro-annuity group argues that in today's uncertain financial world, annuities reduce risk by guaranteeing a lifetime stream of income. Annuity critics contend that investors can set up systematic withdrawal plans from retirement accounts that provide monthly income. While lifetime payments are not guaranteed, a well-diversified portfolio with a modest withdrawal rate can last a lifetime, and still have money left over for an estate.

It really boils down to how much you want to off-load the worry about outliving your savings. If you opt for an annuity, don't jump at the first one offered by a salesman. Do some research and you can save yourself thousands of dollars over the course of your retirement.

SOCIAL SECURITY: WHEN TO START COLLECTING

About 72 percent of those currently receiving Social Security retirement benefits started collecting payments before reaching what the Social Security Administration calls "full retirement age." That's the age at which you can start receiving a full Social Security benefit. Thanks to a commission headed by Alan Greenspan back in 1983, the full retirement age has been rising. The commission's job was to develop proposals to preserve the Social Security program, and their reform package included a combination of tax increases and benefit cuts. One measure gradually delays the age at which people can receive full benefits. Anyone born before 1938 still gets full benefits at the traditional age of 65. For those born in 1938 or later, the full retirement age goes up on a sliding scale, until it reaches age 67 for those born in 1960 or later.

What Is Your Full Retirement Age?

Year of birth	Full retirement age
1937 or earlier	65
1938	65 and 2 months
1939	65 and 4 months
1940	65 and 6 months
1941	65 and 8 months
1942	65 and 10 months
1943–1954	66
1955	66 and 2 months
1956	66 and 4 months
1957	66 and 6 months
1958	66 and 8 months
1959	66 and 10 months
1960 or later	67

As the chart indicates, for the older half of the Boomer generation, 66 is the full retirement age. For younger Boomers, the sliding scale kicks in until 1960. For those born in or after 1960, full retirement age is 67.

Early Retirement

When the Social Security program was established in 1935, retirement benefits began at age 65. In the mid-1950s, women received the right to claim early benefits starting at age 62, an opportunity extended to men in 1961. But under that reform, taking an early benefit meant getting a permanently reduced payment. The idea was to continue giving benefits that, over a lifetime, would be approximately equal for all, regardless of when people start collecting. Those opting for early benefits collect for more years, but get a lower payment. In theory, it all equals out in the end, but in practice, it depends on how long people live to collect benefits.

The Greenspan reforms did not eliminate the option of collecting at age 62, though delaying the full retirement age increased the penalty for taking early benefits. For someone eligible for full retirement at age 66 who starts collecting at age 62, the benefit is 25 percent lower than if they waited until age 66. For those whose full benefits kick in at age 67, collecting at age 62 means a 30 percent reduction in benefits. The benefit reduction works out to about one half of one percent for every month you take benefits in advance of your full retirement age; i.e., start collecting 20 months early and lose about 10 percent of your benefit for life.

Pay Me Now, or Pay Me Later

Whether to start taking benefits early is a personal decision based on individual circumstances. Do you absolutely need the money? Do you have health problems that may shorten your life span? Conversely, do you have a family history of longevity? Do you intend to keep working? All of these factors come into play.

If you don't need the money at age 62 and you expect to live into your late seventies or beyond, then waiting to collect benefits at full retirement age is a better financial strategy.

"If you're feeling lucky and think you are going to be dancing like George Burns until you're 100, then you should postpone taking benefits," says Kurt Czarnowski, regional communications director in the Social Security Administration's Boston office. Czarnowski says many people are caught up in what he calls the Jerry McGuire syndrome of "show me the money." If people take the money as soon as they can, says Czarnowski, "they will shortchange themselves if they live to age 90."

Let's Run the Numbers*

Here is a comparison of two hypothetical Boomers, Fred and Francine, who would each be entitled to a full benefit of $1,500 per month at age 66. Fred can't wait to quit his job and start collecting Social Security at age 62. His reduced benefit is $1,125 per month. By the time Francine collects her first check, Fred has received 48 payments totaling $54,000. When Francine starts collecting, her payments are $375 a month larger than Fred's. It will take 144 months, or 12 years, before Fred and Francine have collected equal amounts. At age 78, Francine starts to pull ahead, and is pleased that she waited until she was eligible to receive her full retirement benefit.

*Analysis does not include adjustments for inflation or time value of money.

Employment Income

Since a large majority of Boomers say they intend to keep working at least into their mid-sixties, taking early Social Security could be a major mistake. Someone collecting early benefits in 2007 can have employment income of just $12,960 or less to avoid a reduction in benefits. Early Social Security payments are trimmed by one dollar for every two dollars of income over the $12,960 limit. For example, if the Social Security recipient makes $25,000, that's $12,040 over the annual limit, resulting in a benefit reduction of $6,020 in 2007. Since the benefit cut for taking early Social Security is permanent, it makes no sense to take early benefits and keep working, unless you expect your income to be below the $12,960 limit. The income limit applies only to work-related income; it does not count pension or investment income. Once you reach full retirement age, you can make as much money as you want without any reduction in benefits.

You Can Change Your Mind

The decision to quit work and start collecting Social Security at age 62 is not irrevocable. For example, if you decide after 10 months of being retired that you would like to go back to work, you can elect to stop receiving benefits. If you then work to full retirement age, your lifetime benefit will be reduced only for the number of months that you collected early benefits. The rate of reduction is about ½ of one percent for each month of receiving early benefits. In this example, the individual who goes back to work after 10 months and then works to full retirement age will see a benefit reduction of about five percent (10 months × ½% per month).

Going Long

While Social Security chops your benefit for dipping in early, they lay on an extra helping if you delay taking benefits beyond full retirement age. Your full benefit goes up by about eight percent a year if you hold off on collecting. You can keep building up credits until age 70, at which point you reach the maximum benefit. For example, a worker entitled to $1,200 a month at age 66 can boost his benefit by some 32 percent if he waits until age 70 to start collecting. That's a nice jump to $1,584 a month. But he had better take good care of himself; it will take until age 82 and a half to break even on the $57,600 he didn't collect between ages 66 and 70. Of the 30 million people receiving Social Security retirement benefits, only about 4 million have any credits for working beyond full retirement age.

Your Social Security Statement

The Social Security Administration sends out annual statements to taxpayers with details of their estimated benefits and earnings history. It is a very helpful report, but it may not accurately reflect your future plans. The report assumes that you will continue to work to full retirement age, and that future income will be about the same as it has been in recent years. But what if you plan to retire early, or throttle back on your hours and income? How would that affect your Social Security payments?

You can get your own customized Social Security Statement with whatever scenario you choose. "You can request one any time you want and build it using different assumptions," says Social Security's Kurt Czarnowski. "If you want to find out the impact of going part-time at age 58, you can request a Social Security statement that includes those assumptions. You can submit several forms with different scenarios. It's a no-cost service that we provide, and we want people to take advantage of it."

You can apply for a statement online or ask that an application be mailed to you. Questions 7 and 8 on the application ask at what age you plan to stop working, and what you expect your future average earnings to be. With that information, Social Security can provide a more accurate estimate of your benefits. You will receive your new statement within two to four weeks. The Social Security Administration website is www.socialsecurity.gov.

11

LIVING ON LESS

"A penny saved is a penny earned." It is one of Benjamin Franklin's best-known sayings. It was sage advice, but old Ben gave that tip long before state and federal income taxes and FICA withholding. Depending on your tax situation, you may have to earn $1.35 to have one dollar in take-home pay. If you clip a coupon and save one dollar on a purchase, it has the same effect as going out and earning $1.35. These days, a penny saved beats a penny earned.

This chapter looks at many ways to cut costs and save money, both before and during retirement. Building up a nice cushion of retirement savings is Plan A, but if that falls short, living on less is the cornerstone of Plan B. For the vast majority of Boomers who are still working, trimming expenses can free up cash to boost savings or pay down debt. Once retired, lower living costs can stretch retirement savings further.

Cutting costs can involve minor nips and tucks, like taking your own lunch to work, or a major lifestyle overhaul, such as moving to a lower cost part of the country. Some cost savings may come easily, almost naturally. Many Boomers are finding that material things no longer provide much satisfaction. A generation known for its conspicuous consumption may now be moving toward a more reflective path. We find that the most meaningful times in our lives involve family and friends, and simple activities like hiking, cooking a meal together, or reading a good book. When we splurge, it is more likely on an experience, like travel, than on a plasma TV or some other big-ticket item.

"We look at this mass of junk that we've accumulated, and we've spent a lot of money on it, and it's really not worth anything to us," says nationally recognized financial planner Deena Katz, CFP, of Evensky and Katz in Coral Gables, Florida. She says Boomers "are finding value in things that are more natural. We are finding value in our family relationships, value in our community relationships. That's bringing us a whole new dimension to the next phase of life."

With more of a focus on relationships and experiences and less on material possessions, Boomers can cut costs and still find fulfillment. Katz thinks Boomers will turn frugality into a new status symbol. "I'm hearing a lot of Boomers say, 'I don't need an SUV. It eats a lot of gas. It's not that I can't afford one'—though they probably can't—'I think I'll get something a little more economical, and it gets me where I want to go. I'll walk sometimes because I need the exercise, and I want to be physically fit.' So all of these things are working together to convince us that a simpler lifestyle is a better lifestyle; that we don't need to amass a lot of accoutrements that are valueless and meaningless outside of purchasing them."

BIG APPLE TO THE LITTLE APPLE

"The baby Boomers have a BMW lifestyle, but they don't have much in the bank," says former *New York Times* financial columnist Fred Brock. "But Boomers being Boomers, they are going to change the rules of the game. They are going to adjust their lifestyles to match the money they have, and that's going to be their second act. They are going to go places where they can continue to learn, continue to work and be vital."

Fred Brock thinks many Boomers are going to move to lower-cost communities across America. "The Boomers are a stressed-out generation," he says. "They want to downsize. They want to go to smaller towns; they want a simpler life, a less complicated life." On that front, Brock is a pioneer. He and his wife moved from Montclair, New Jersey, a suburb of New York City, to Manhattan, Kansas, where Fred teaches at Kansas State University. Friends say they went from "the Big Apple" to "the Little Apple," the nickname for Manhattan, Kansas.

Switching apples took a nice bite out of the cost of living. Brock, author of several personal finance books, including *Retire on Less Than You Think*, sold his home in New Jersey with enough profit to buy a house for cash in Kansas and still have money left over. "And it's a much bigger, much nicer house," says Brock. "So we essentially bought a house that's much bigger for about half the price of what we sold our house for in New Jersey." He says annual property taxes dropped from $9,000 a year to $2,700. Car insurance, for two vehicles, went from $3,000 in New Jersey to around $700 in Kansas. "When you cut expenses, you increase your income. That's the bottom line," says Brock.

"The financial advantages of moving from a very expensive area like New York or San Francisco to a less expensive area are staggering," says Brock. "So the Boomers are going to be able to sell their properties in these places, and move to much less expensive areas, where they can probably buy a house outright, and have no mortgage. And believe me, living without a mortgage makes your life much simpler and much less expensive."

Brock recognizes that many Boomers want to "age in place." People often have deep roots in their communities. Family ties, friendships, church affiliations, and the familiarity and comfort of feeling at home are all good reasons to stay put. Brock says a small-scale version of his "Manhattan transfer" could still save money. "If a New Yorker wanted to retire but stay generally in the New York area," says Brock, "they could move to someplace like eastern Pennsylvania, which is maybe an hour and half away from New York City. So you are still a reasonable driving distance, yet you are in a place like Bethlehem, Pennsylvania, or Allentown, Pennsylvania, where the cost of living is way below New York City."

These strategies will not work for everyone. While the East and West Coasts of the U.S. saw huge appreciation in real estate prices in the late '90s and early 2000s, much of the rest of the country did not. Selling a house in Indiana will probably not finance a move to south Florida. Housing markets go through up and down cycles. Some Boomers may hit the real estate jackpot; others may not. It is risky to count too heavily on rising real estate values to finance your retirement. The gains may not happen, or you may not want to move to some faraway place, just because it's relatively cheap. It's best to keep saving for retirement, and if a real estate windfall comes through, it makes your retirement security that much better.

Crunching the Numbers

For those thinking about relocating to other parts of the country, websites can help with the financial calculations. Can you live on less in Phoenix, Arizona, than you can in Burlington, Vermont? The answer is yes. It costs about 14 percent less to live in Phoenix than Burlington, according to a cost of living comparison calculator at Bankrate.com. The calculator compares the prices of housing, food, clothing, medical care, entertainment, repair services, and more to show the financial impact of moving from one city to another. Here are some examples:

If you live on $75,000 a year in . . .	And you are considering moving to . . .	The same standard of living will cost . . .
Appleton, WI	Ft. Smith, AR	$67,072
Hartford, CT	Norman, OK	60,245
Lexington, KY	Mobile, AL	70,241
New York City (Manhattan)	Spartanburg, SC	33,382
San Diego, CA	Bellingham, WA	51,546

You can see that the cost of living varies widely. The New York City to Spartanburg move looks inviting. The biggest difference is that the average apartment in New York costs about $1,000,000, while you can get a nice house in Spartanburg for $225,000. The Web address for the calculator is www.bankrate.com/brm/movecalc.asp.

SMART WAYS TO SAVE MONEY

Many people say they have a hard time saving money. While it is difficult to save big chunks of money all at once, it is relatively simple to shave a few dollars off routine expenses on an ongoing basis. Over time, those little savings add up. There are many newsletters and websites for people who practically make a religion out of living on the cheap. We are not fanatics about this, but we have been collecting money-saving tips for years. Here are a number of suggestions for cutting expenses, which do not require adopting a "live so tight it squeaks" lifestyle.

Home

- Ask your insurance agent to look for a lower cost home owner's policy. It's a competitive area, but most people just stick with what they have, year after year. If you switch, make sure the new insurer is financially sound.
- Ask how much you can save by increasing the deductible on your home owner's policy. You may save 25 percent on your premium by increasing your deductible from $500 to $1,000, according to the Insurance Information Institute.
- You may be able to get a lower home owner's insurance premium if you have a security system, a dead bolt lock, and if nobody in the household smokes.
- If you are at least 55 years old and retired, you may qualify for an insurance discount of up to 10 percent at some companies. The risk of burglary drops in homes that are occupied most of the time.
- If you refinance your mortgage, avoid variable-rate loans. Why take on that uncertainty? Don't keep refinancing with 30-year mortgages or you'll never live mortgage-free. Fifteen-year mortgages have lower interest rates, and allow you to "burn the mortgage" sooner.

- Energy Star appliances cost more up front, but save on energy in the long run. With high energy prices, the payback time is faster. They are better for the environment, too.
- Compact fluorescent lightbulbs (CFLs) create as much light as an incandescent bulb but use one-quarter to one-sixth as much electricity, and they last 10 to 15 times longer.
- Install a programmable thermostat and set it to follow your family's normal routine. It allows you to adjust the time and temperature settings of your furnace according to a preset schedule.
- Arrange for a professional to perform a home energy audit to determine your home's energy efficiency. Use weather stripping, insulate hot water pipes, and install precut insulation gaskets around electrical switches and outlet plates on exterior walls.
- Have your furnace serviced annually by a qualified contractor to ensure safety and maximum energy efficiency. Change or clean filters on the furnace as needed.

Auto

- When purchasing a new car, do online research on prices and options. Before buying, check prices with four or five dealers. One may be anxious to make a deal, and you can save hundreds of dollars.
- Unless a car dealer is offering special low-rate financing, don't jump at dealership financing plans. You are buying a financial service (a loan) as well as a car. Shop for both.
- When buying a car, consider the total cost including insurance, gas, and maintenance. For details, check out the Consumer Reports new car guide at the public library.
- Trading in a car for a new one every three or four years is very expensive. Keep your car well maintained and drive it for as long as you can. Once car payments are finished, set aside that monthly payment in a savings account.

- Consider buying a certified pre-owned car instead of a new one.
- Be an informed consumer. When trading in a car or buying a used car, look up the Blue Book value of the car.
- Have a mechanic check out a used car before you buy it.
- For older cars, consider dropping collision and/or comprehensive insurance coverage altogether. Paying an extra $250 to protect something worth just $1,000 doesn't make sense.
- Some companies offer discounts to drivers who have three or more years without an accident or moving violation. See if you qualify.
- In some cases, an insurance company may offer a multi-policy discount if a consumer purchases both auto and home owners' coverage.
- Ask about discounts for cars equipped with safety features, such as antilock brakes, antitheft devices, and automatic seat belts.
- If you stop commuting by car, you may qualify for a low-mileage discount on your auto insurance.
- Before renting a car and paying excessive insurance fees, ask your insurance agent if your auto policy extends to rental cars. Some credit cards also provide car rental insurance coverage, if you use the card for the rental.
- If you have a young driver on your auto insurance policy who is away at school, ask your agent if you can get a reduced premium because your child is away for most of the year.
- Drivers over the age of 50, who tend to be more cautious than younger drivers, may be eligible for reduced rates.
- Use low octane gasoline unless the manufacturer recommends otherwise.
- Keep an eye out for gas stations with low prices, and plan fill-ups accordingly.
- Properly inflated tires give you better gas mileage.
- Driving the speed limit uses less gas.
- Use public transportation.

Food

- We know you have heard about taking your own lunch to work, but have you calculated the savings? Let's say it costs $2 to make your own lunch versus $6 to buy one at work, a $4 savings. If it takes five minutes to pack a lunch, it's like being paid at a rate of $48 an hour to slap lunch meat on bread. It could be the highest paid work you do all day!

- Eat breakfast at home, or at least brew your own coffee, make some toast, and take it with you. Better than buying coffee and a donut for $2.

- If you spend $1 a day buying soda at work, bring in your own can and put it in the office fridge. You'll save 75 cents a day or $15 a month (assuming no one swipes the can).

- Before food shopping, plan the trip. Look for bargains in the store circular, if available. Make a shopping list and retrieve coupons for items on the list. A few minutes of advance planning can lead to hefty savings at the checkout.

- When a big sale hits on items you use often, stock up. If short of cupboard space, store items under the bed.

- Don't shop when your stomach is growling. Hungry shoppers get trigger-happy and buy more food than they need. People tend to buy more junk food when they are delirious with hunger pains.

- When stocking up at a food warehouse, don't buy a 50-pound bag of cookies just because it's a bargain. It just means the family gets fat eating more cookies than usual. Bulk buying works best for staples you will use at a normal rate, like tuna fish or paper towels.

- Buying a large size usually means a lower unit price, but not always. Check prices carefully. Avoid buying large quantities that end up being spoiled and thrown out.

- Save the cost of an expensive dinner out by inviting friends to a potluck supper where everybody brings a dish.

- If the budget is tight, consider cooking up something special as a gift instead of splurging at the mall. The personal touch can make a present even more special.

Health

- Ask your doctor to prescribe generic drugs when possible.
- If you take regular medication, use a mail-order prescription service to get a 90-day supply. This cuts down on copayments.
- If your health plan offers a reimbursement for gym membership, fill out the paperwork and send it in on time. Many plans reimburse up to $150 a year.
- If self-employed, consider getting a lower cost health plan with high deductibles, and using tax-advantaged Health Savings Accounts to pay for out-of-pocket expenses. (More on this in chapter 12.)
- Self-employed individuals or small-business owners may be able to obtain a lower group-rate premium if they purchase health insurance as members of a trade association or local chamber of commerce.

Financial Services

- Always shop around for loans. Don't sign up just because someone called you or sent you a solicitation in the mail. Do some legwork, get the best rate, and enjoy the savings month after month.
- Term life insurance is usually the best buy. If you buy whole life or variable life, plan to hold on to the policy for at least 10 to 15 years. Payments in the early years go toward commissions. If you drop out too soon you will have very little savings accumulated.
- Don't be late on credit card payments. The card companies make tons of money slapping people with late fees and jacking up rates if they pay late. A late payment on one card can result

in a higher rate on other cards, as well. (They share the dirty secrets.)

- Don't just make the minimum payment on credit cards. Minimum payment schedules keep you on the hook for years, making very slow progress on retiring the debt.
- If you carry a balance, pay your credit card bill when it arrives rather than just before the due date. You are charged interest based on your daily balance. There is no point in having money sitting in your checking account earning no interest when it could be reducing a card balance with a 17 percent interest rate.
- Transfer balances to lower-rate cards, but be sure to understand any transaction fees that might be charged.
- If you usually carry a credit card balance, shop for cards with the lowest rates. If you pay cards off each month, look for cards with the best perks, even if they have high interest rates (which will not affect you if you keep paying in full).
- Close credit accounts you do not need. Having too many open accounts can affect your credit rating and result in higher interest rates for loans.
- Sign up for the Upromise program. A percentage of many credit card purchases goes into a college savings fund for your children or grandchildren. The website is www.upromise.com.
- Look for free checking with the lowest required minimum balance. Most banks pay little, if any, interest on checking accounts. Keeping a minimum of $2,500 or $5,000 in the bank means not earning a decent rate of interest on that money. That's the equivalent of paying for checking.
- Plan to make ATM withdrawals from your own bank to avoid costly and annoying fees from using other ATMs.
- Pay bills online. Save postage, cost of checks and envelopes, and trips to the post office.
- Use no-load mutual funds. Consider using index funds, which have much lower management fees than actively managed funds.

- Many employees get a generous tax break using Flexible Spending Accounts (FSA) at work to pay for child care and out-of-pocket medical costs. Ask your human resources department for details.
- Find out if you have money owed to you from an old savings account, insurance payment, dividend check, or security deposit. Locate your state's unclaimed property through the National Association of Unclaimed Property Administrators' website at www.unclaimed.org.

Retail/Services/Entertainment

- Review phone bills to see if you are paying for services you don't use. We discovered we were paying $10 a month for extras we didn't use or want.
- See if you can drop your landline and just use your mobile phone. Why do we pay for two services that do the same thing?
- Look at your cable TV bill to see if you are paying for channels you don't watch. It takes time to check this out, but if you discover a way to cut the charge, you enjoy the savings month after month.
- Stop buying clothes that are dry-clean only. Iron clothing while you watch TV. At $1.25 per shirt, save $5.00 watching a half-hour sitcom.
- Sell stuff you don't need or use on eBay.
- Shop resale shops, estate sales, and clearance racks.
- Don't renew subscriptions to publications you don't have time to read.
- Use the public library to check out movies or books free.
- Give up expensive health club memberships. Exercise outdoors or at home. Or join the YMCA.
- Wash your car at home and save $10.
- Avoid shopping as entertainment. Take a walk.

- Don't buy extended warranty contracts. Most are never used by consumers. Home electronics and appliances usually come with a basic warranty, and if the product is a lemon, it often shows up within the warranty period.
- Do not shop with big-spending friends. They will encourage you to buy things that are too expensive, that you would otherwise be able to pass up.
- Before you buy any expensive discretionary item, wait 24 hours. The urge may pass.
- Go to a matinee instead of movies at night.
- Have cocktails at home and then go out to dinner. Come home for dessert.
- Travel just before or after peak season to get better rates on flights and hotels. This works especially well for empty nesters who can avoid travel during school vacations.

Coupons to Cash: Clip Smart to Save More

Shoppers save around $3 billion a year by redeeming coupons. The industry trade association says three out of four U.S. shoppers use coupons. Clipping and organizing coupons is an investment in time and effort. Here are some clipping tips to stretch coupons a little further:

- Plan to spend 15 to 20 minutes clipping Sunday paper coupons with the goal of saving $5 to $10.
- Get a file to organize coupons by product categories. File the earliest expiration coupons in the front of each category. Clear out expired coupons.
- Call company 800 numbers and ask for coupons. Many manufacturers will mail coupons if requested. Coupons are also available online at sites such as www.coolsavings.com.
- Before shopping, go through the file to select coupons for use that day. Plan a menu around coupon items.

Coupon Do's and Don'ts

- Do stock up when items can be stored and will not spoil. Don't use coupons to buy multiple packages of high fat or sugar foods. When that stuff is around in large quantities, it is eaten more quickly. Bad for waistline and budget.
- Do look for coupons that can be used at drug stores, restaurants, and other retailers. More outlets are using this form of promotion.
- Don't buy an expensive brand just because there is a coupon. A cheaper alternative may be a better buy even with the coupon savings off the high-priced product.

Coupon Resources

For more information on the smart use of coupons, visit a website run by the Promotion Marketing Association Coupon Council at www.couponmonth.com. For information on using coupons to feed the hungry, go to www.cutouthunger.org.

CAPTURE THE SAVINGS

If you save a few dollars on lunch or ironing your own pants, you are not likely to go to the bank with eight bucks and make a deposit. If you leave the money hanging around in your wallet, you will be tempted to spend it on something else. The best way to capture the savings is to make a commitment to save a certain extra amount each month. It could be $100 or $200 or more. Then have that money taken directly from your checking account and invested in a mutual fund. Or, take that much more out of your paycheck and put it in your 401(k). The saving is done up front automatically, and then you can pan for gold with all these savings tips so you'll never even miss the cash you added to savings. If you save an extra $200 a month earning a seven percent rate of return, you'll build up $14,300 in 5 years. Keep it up for 10 years and you'll sock away $34,600.

Saving money takes some effort. But look at it as a part-time job that pays you in tax-free dollars. Most of the suggestions above will not affect your lifestyle, but they can generate savings that will enhance your standard of living in the next phase of your life.

Part Five

HEALTH

12

BRIDGING THE
HEALTH CARE GAP

A friend of ours is about to make a major life change. When he turns 60 in a few months, he plans to quit his job in New York and move to Colorado to live with his longtime significant other. He plans to do some work in Colorado, but he may never work in a full-time job with benefits again. It's a big decision, made even more challenging by what to do about health insurance. Because he does not qualify for Medicare for another five years, he has to find and pay for his own insurance. It's a dilemma shared by a growing number of Boomers.

With the rising cost of health insurance and the risks of being without coverage, that gap prior to age 65 is becoming a major impediment. It keeps some people stuck in jobs they would like to leave. It discourages would-be entrepreneurs from retiring to start new businesses. Some people continue working beyond age 65 so their benefits will cover a younger spouse who does not yet qualify for Medicare. This health care "job lock" is freezing movement in the workplace, frustrating midlife workers ready to move on, and preventing younger employees from advancing into positions that would otherwise be vacated.

It's the price we pay for being the only major industrialized country not to have national health insurance, under which citizens are covered regardless of employment status. In our increasingly global economy, U.S. companies are hampered by ever-rising medical expenses. The big automakers pay more per vehicle in health care costs than they do for steel. Small businesses, the true engine of job growth in America, are staggering under the weight of health care costs, and many are dropping or reducing coverage. As a result, the number of uninsured Americans keeps rising. We are experiencing a meltdown of the employer-based health benefit system in the U.S. It's only a matter of time until it disintegrates to the point where we will have the political will to fix it. Until then, we have to muddle through.

Adding to the problem for Boomers is the number of companies discontinuing health care benefits for retirees. A Kaiser/Hewitt survey found that between 1988 and 2005, the share of employers with 200 or more employees offering retiree health benefits declined from 66 percent to 33 percent. Such benefits are rare among smaller firms. The U.S. Agency for Healthcare Research and Quality estimates that one in four people ages 51 to 57 will be without health insurance at some point before becoming eligible for Medicare. During his second term, President Clinton proposed a Medicare "buy-in" plan to allow people between ages 55 and 64 to purchase Medicare coverage at reasonable rates. The proposal failed.

So, what's a Boomer to do? We examine three possibilities for those losing, by choice or by force, the security of employer-provided health benefits:

- COBRA continuation of coverage
- Purchasing insurance in the open market
- High deductible health plans coupled with Health Savings Accounts

DEFANGING COBRA

If you are puzzled as to why a health insurance benefit is named after a deadly snake, that's understandable. You can blame Congress. The benefit was included in legislation titled the *Consolidated Omnibus Budget Reconciliation Act* of 1986, or COBRA. Employers with 20 or more workers in a group plan are covered by the act.

The law says that a worker who leaves a job for any reason other than gross misconduct is entitled to purchase a temporary continuation of group health insurance benefits. COBRA also protects employees who lose health coverage because of a reduction in hours. The worker and his or her spouse and children can receive coverage for up to 18 months; it can be extended beyond that under some circumstances. There are no waiting periods or exclusions for preexisting conditions. The law entitles workers to buy coverage at the employer's group plan rate, plus two percent in administrative fees. Since the employer is no longer paying for any of the benefits the monthly premium is expensive, but the group rate is generally a bargain compared to buying a policy in the open market.

When one of us left a job recently, we received the standard COBRA notification that is required by law. The monthly premium quoted for the two of us and a college-age daughter was $928 for an HMO. Two years before that we had to purchase coverage in the open market for a stretch, and the rate was $1,207 per month. (A similar plan in 2007 is $1,402 per month.) These are Boston area prices, which tend to be among the highest in the nation.

You have a 60-day window in which to sign up for coverage under COBRA. After leaving your job, you will be mailed a packet of COBRA documents. Read the materials carefully, and follow up with phone calls if there is any confusion. Your COBRA application must be postmarked by the end of the 60 days, or you waive your right to coverage. You have 45 days after electing coverage to pay the premiums due. Even though you might not sign up for COBRA until weeks after you have left a job, the coverage is retroactive to the day after your prior coverage ended.

Snakebit Despite COBRA

Here is a personal story from our own experience about how COBRA can't always protect you. Mark was working for a radio station in Boston whose owner also ran a financial planning business. Everyone came into work one day and discovered that the boss had been stealing millions of dollars from his clients for years, had admitted his crimes in recorded messages, and had attempted to commit suicide. In short order, the radio station and financial planning business were shut down, and the group health plan was cancelled. Continued health benefits were unavailable. The simple explanation: If there is no longer a health plan, there is no COBRA coverage available. The suicide attempt failed and the pilfering financial planner is now serving time in federal prison.

The U.S. Department of Labor website has extensive information on the inner workings of COBRA. The link is painfully long: www.dol.gov/dol/topic/health-plans/cobra.htm. You can also just do a Web search for COBRA. Along with a few snake websites, the Department of Labor page appears near the top of the listings.

GETTING HIP TO HIPAA

The *Health Insurance Portability and Accountability Act* of 1996, or HIPAA, is best known for its provisions on medical records and privacy. However, it also has a section that guarantees access to health insurance, which may be invaluable to Boomers trying to plug the insurance gap in the drive toward the Medicare goal line.

First, some background. One problem with going off on your own and purchasing health insurance is that you may be denied coverage. In most states, health insurance companies can turn you down if they think your medical history makes you a risky bet. The road to better profits is to pay as few claims as possible. With group policies, insurers are generally stuck with anybody a company hires. However, with individual policies, they exercise much more discretion. If you have a history of high cholesterol, high blood pressure, diabetes, or some other ailment, your application for an individual policy may be turned down.

This is where HIPAA comes in. HIPAA guarantees access to individual health insurance policies, regardless of preexisting conditions, if:

- You have had health insurance for the last 18 months without any break in coverage of 63 days or more, and you were covered by a group plan at the end of that 18-month period.
- You received benefits under COBRA but have exhausted your coverage.
- You are not eligible for COBRA (e.g., company has fewer than 20 employees).
- You are not eligible for another group health plan, Medicare, or Medicaid.

All carriers that sell individual health care policies in your state must offer their two most marketed individual plans to HIPAA-eligible individuals, regardless of health status. Coverage under HIPAA is expensive, but it can guarantee you access to health insurance until you reach Medicare eligibility. You must sign up for coverage under HIPAA within 63 days of the expiration of your prior coverage. For more information on how to buy individual health insurance coverage under HIPAA, contact your state department of insurance.

PREEXISTING CONDITIONS AND "BREAKS IN COVERAGE"

With group health plans, insurance companies cannot refuse coverage, but they can impose a "preexisting condition" clause that denies coverage for up to 12 months for certain medical problems. Preexisting conditions are those for which medical advice, diagnosis, or treatment was recommended or received within six months of your policy enrollment date. (That's the first day of your coverage, or, if there is a waiting period, your date of hire.) However, that 12-month exclusion can be reduced or eliminated if you had prior health insurance without a "break in coverage" of 63 days or more. The exclusion period is shortened by one day for every day of prior coverage. If you were covered for at least the past 12 months without a 63-day break, the preexisting condition clause is lifted.

When you leave a health insurance plan, the insurance company must send you a certificate showing proof of the dates of your coverage. The form also explains your rights under HIPAA. A break in coverage of 63 days or more invalidates all prior coverage in determining how much of a preexisting condition period applies to you.

WHAT'S YOUR STATE OF HEALTH?

The state where you reside can affect your rights to health insurance coverage. We have described the minimum protections available to all citizens under federal law. Some states have standards that are more consumer friendly. Underscoring the lack of a national health insurance system, the states have a checkerboard of rules and regulations that govern the health insurance rights of citizens. As of 2007, five states have "guaranteed-issue" laws that require all health insurers that offer individual policies to sell standardized products to all applicants. In other words, you cannot be denied an individual policy because of a preexisting condition. Those states are Maine, Massachusetts, New Jersey, New York, and Vermont. Individual policies are generally more expensive in these states because the insurers can't weed out the bad risks.

Thirty-four states offer some form of high-risk pool, covering about 183,000 people, according to the Health Insurance Resource Center. These plans create a pool out of all the people that private insurance companies do not want to sell policies to, and then provide a state-sponsored health insurance plan the individuals can buy into, though at a higher price than a typical individual policy. A good source of information on health insurance questions, including high-risk pools, is the website at healthinsurance.org. On the home page look for a link to "information on high-risk insurance pools."

Eleven states have no high-risk pool option, according to a Kaiser Family Foundation website (statehealthfacts.org). This means if you are denied an individual policy because of a preexisting condition and are not covered under COBRA or HIPAA, you may not be able to obtain health insurance. Those states are Arizona, Delaware, Georgia, Hawaii, Michigan, Nevada, North Carolina, Ohio, Pennsylvania, Rhode Island, and Virginia. However, the patchwork of state laws applies here, as well. Some of these states do have limited provisions for people to buy individual policies. In Michigan, for example, Blue Cross Blue Shield must sell individual health insurance to any resident. You can check the rules in your state through a website run by the Georgetown University Health Policy Institute at www.health-insuranceinfo.net.

"A preexisting condition can make it extremely difficult—often impossible—to get coverage under an individual policy," writes former *New York Times* columnist Fred Brock in his book *Health Care on Less Than You Think.* If you live in a place where you end up without any health insurance options, you may have to move to another state where you can obtain coverage. Now that's a sad state of affairs.

BUYING IN THE OPEN MARKET

If you have to go shopping for your own individual policy, your experience in selecting health plans at work will help, but the decision will be much more complex. You may have many more options available, and you will have to tailor your choice to your particular budget and health care needs. You will be entering a marketplace that is highly fragmented. An industry trade association, America's Health Insurance Plans, claims nearly 1,300 member companies providing health insurance to more than 200 million Americans. But most companies do not offer coverage in all 50 states. They have different product offerings with a wide variety of provisions. Making apples-to-apples comparisons can be a daunting challenge. Rates vary by geographic region and age of the applicant. Some insurers may turn you down for a preexisting condition while others may not. Some policies have all the bells and whistles; some are bare bones, at best. As a rule, the more protection you want, the more you will have to pay.

A DEFINING MOMENT

Before we begin comparison shopping for health care policies, let's take a moment to define some of the terms you need to know. This is definitely one of those "you can't tell the players without a scorecard" situations. Getting a feel for the terminology will help you to make an informed choice.

Deductible: The amount of your health care costs that you must pay before the insurance plan starts paying any bills. For example, you may be responsible for the first $1,000 in health costs before the insurance kicks in.

Copayments: Charges that you and the insurance company split. Usually, your share is smaller. You might have a $30 copayment for a doctor's visit that costs $120.

Coinsurance: The amount you must pay for medical care services after you have met the plan's copayments and deductibles. For example, if your insurance company covers 80 percent of a medical charge, you are required to cover the remaining 20 percent as coinsurance.

Out-of-pocket limit: The outside limit of what you might have to pay in a year. For example, if your policy stipulates 20 percent coinsurance for surgery, and you have an operation that costs $25,000, you would theoretically owe $5,000 for the procedure. But if your "out-of-pocket" limit is $2,000, you would not be required to pay beyond that limit. In some policies, the out-of-pocket limit is in addition to the deductible.

Lifetime maximum: The most that a plan will pay in total claims in your lifetime. With the rising cost of medical care, and the monumental expense of certain operations and treatments, this is an important figure to consider. Look for plans with a limit of at least $1 million. You may be more comfortable with a $3 million or $5 million limit.

Health Maintenance Organization (HMO): Health plans that generally have lower out-of-pocket health care expenses but place more restrictions on your choice of doctors or hospitals than other health insurance plans. HMO members must choose a primary care physician (PCP), and get a referral from that physician before seeing any specialists. Most HMO plans have modest copayments, and no deductibles or coinsurance. HMOs attempt to lower costs by encouraging regular checkups and preventive care.

Preferred Provider Organization (PPO): A health plan in which patients are encouraged to use the insurance company's network of preferred doctors and hospitals. These health care providers have been contracted to deliver services at a discounted rate. You do not have to choose a primary care physician to coordinate your care, and you are free to use specialists within the network. Most plans have an annual deductible and copayments. If a doctor outside of the network treats you, insurance will cover a smaller percentage of the charges than for network doctors.

LET'S GO SHOPPING

To provide insight into selecting a health insurance plan, we present examples of three plans that were available in April 2007. The plans were found through the website at www.ehealthinsurance.com. We performed a hypothetical search for individual health coverage for two single Boomers and for a married couple. All the applicants are nonsmokers and are in good health:

- Fifty-nine-year-old single woman in Denver, Colorado
- Sixty-two-year-old single man in Chicago, Illinois
- Married couple: man age 63, woman age 59, in Raleigh, North Carolina

	Plan A
Policy Applicants	59-year-old single woman, Denver, CO
Name of Plan	Kaiser Permanente $30 copayment plan
Type	HMO
Financial Rating	B++ (Very good)
Monthly Premium	$351.31
Deductible	None
Coinsurance	None
Out-of-Pocket Limit	$3000
Doctor Visit	$30 copay
Prescriptions	Not covered
ER	$150
Outpatient Surgery	$150
Hospitalization	20% coinsurance per admission
Lifetime Maximum	No lifetime maximum Transplant lifetime maximum $1,000,000 per individual

Plan B	Plan C
62-year-old single man, Chicago, IL	63-year-old man and 59-year-old woman, Raleigh, NC
Blue Cross Blue Shield of Illinois Select Blue $1000/80%	Celtic Basic PPO 80/20 Plan
PPO	PPO
A+ (Superior)	A- (Excellent)
$588.92	$586.98
$1000	Family: $5000/$2500 per person
20% after deductible	20% after deductible
$1000 not including deductible	Family: $9000/$4500 per person, including deductible
$20 copay	$30 copay for two visits, then 20% coinsurance after deductible
20% coinsurance after deductible	$1000 deductible, then generic $25 copay; brand 35% coinsurance
No charge—deductible waived	$250 additional deductible per visit (waived if admitted)
20% coinsurance after deductible	$250 additional deductible per occurrence, 20% coinsurance after deductible
20% coinsurance after deductible	$500 additional deductible per admission, 20% coinsurance after deductible
$5 million	$5 million per person

For the fifty-nine-year-old Denver woman, 87 plans were available with monthly premiums ranging from $170.29 to $728.90.

The sixty-two-year-old man from Chicago could choose from among 98 plans ranging in price from $177.26 to $1,276.34 per month.

The couple in Raleigh, North Carolina, man age 63 and woman age 59, had a choice of 66 plans with monthly premiums ranging from $351.20 to $1,583.98.

The more expensive plans have low deductibles, modest copayments, generous prescription benefits, low out-of-pocket limits, and high lifetime protection.

Plan Analysis

Plan A is an HMO policy for a fifty-nine-year-old single woman in Denver. There is no deductible, so the insurance takes effect right away. She pays just $30 for a doctor's appointment, but gets no prescription coverage. If she is taking a regular medication, that provision may cause her to look elsewhere. If hospitalized, she pays coinsurance of 20 percent of the cost per admission. But her annual out-of-pocket maximum is $3,000, which gives her protection against a medical catastrophe. The plan has no lifetime maximum.

Kaiser Permanente is a large and reputable health insurance provider. It has a B++, or "very good" rating from A.M. Best, which analyzes an insurer's financial strength and ability to meet ongoing obligations to policyholders.

For someone in good health, who expects just routine doctor visits and does not take expensive medications, this plan is attractive. The premium of $351.31 is reasonable, and her routine care requires just a moderate copayment.

Plan B is a PPO policy for a sixty-two-year-old single man in Chicago. He is not required to have a primary care physician, and needs no referral to see specialists within the PPO network. He has a deductible of $1,000, but that does not apply to doctor's visits, which carry a $20 copay. The deductible does apply to prescriptions, outpatient surgery, and hospital admissions, as does a 20 percent coinsurance provision. The annual out-of-pocket limit is $1,000, plus the deductible of $1,000. The lifetime maximum is generous at $5 million. Blue Cross Blue Shield of Illinois has a "superior" A+ rating from A.M. Best.

The premium of $588.92 per month works out to more than $7,000 a year, which is high for one person. But the low doctor copayment, prescription coverage, and the $2,000 maximum in annual charges provide good protection. At 62, age is a factor. The same policy for a fifty-eight-year-old is $116 per month less.

Plan C is a PPO policy for a couple in Raleigh, North Carolina. The man is 63 and his wife is 59. It's a basic plan with a monthly premium of $586.98, lower than the single man in Chicago is paying for his coverage. The deductible is $2,500 per person. If one person reaches that limit, insurance will kick in for him or her, even if the other spouse has not yet met his or her deductible. Coinsurance is 20 percent after the deductible has been met.

The out-of-pocket annual limit is $4,500 per person, including the deductible, which means $2,000 in additional spending over the deductible limit. The first two doctor visits have a $30 copay; after that, they have to pay until reaching the deductible, and then still pay 20 percent coinsurance beyond the deductible. If they go to the emergency room or have outpatient surgery, $250 is added on to their deductible per event. And if they are hospitalized their deductible goes up by $500 per admission. The $5 million lifetime limit per person is a plus. Celtic Health Insurance, a nationwide company based in Chicago, has an A.M. Best rating of A–, which is "excellent."

At just over $7,000 a year, this is moderately priced insurance for two people, ages 63 and 59. But the plan certainly lives up to its name as "basic." This is a plan for people in good health who do not take expensive prescriptions. The rising deductibles for trips to the ER, surgery, and hospital stays are a drawback. The $4,500 per person out-of-pocket limit is a backstop against disaster, but if you just have a rough year with a trip to the ER, a surgery, and several rounds of medication, you are going to take a big hit, in addition to the $7,000 in premiums. The couple in Raleigh can find a more generous policy, but it could cost hundreds of dollars more per month.

WILL YOU QUALIFY FOR AN INDIVIDUAL HEALTH PLAN?

If you have always had jobs with group benefits and took for granted that you would be eligible for health insurance, you enter a different zone when applying for an individual policy. Except for a handful of states where all applicants must be accepted, you can be denied coverage for a preexisting condition. (See earlier descriptions of COBRA, HIPAA, and state laws under which you may have a right to obtain coverage.)

When you apply for health insurance, the insurance company examines how much of a risk you are through a process called "underwriting." This is a major factor in determining whether they offer you coverage, how much they will charge, and whether they may exclude coverage for specific ailments. Here is how one major health insurance company explains underwriting on its website:

> "Your health plan application is individually underwritten based on the health history of you and your covered dependents. To effectively underwrite your application, we must obtain as much medical information about you as possible. This is accomplished through the use of health questions on the application form and, in some instances, a follow-up medical questionnaire and/or telephone verification of information. In addition, we may request medical records as necessary."

The company may accept your application at the standard premium rate, or reject you entirely. Other possibilities include the following:

- Provide full protection but with a higher premium
- Modify the benefits to increase the deductible
- Exclude a specific medical problem from coverage

A major study in 2004 by America's Health Insurance Plans (AHIP) showed the percentage of applications by age groups that were accepted or rejected. Eighty percent of applicants ages 50 to 54 were offered coverage. For applicants ages 55 to 59, 75 percent were offered coverage. And for the 60 to 64 age group, 70 percent received an offer of coverage. However, a significant number of the offers were for coverage at higher than the standard premium, or with limits on what medical problems would be covered.

With those numbers factored in, a majority of the fifty- to sixty-four-year-olds did not get an offer of coverage at the standard rate. Of those in the 50 to 54 age group, 53 percent of original applicants got accepted with the standard rate. That dropped to 45 percent in the 55 to 59 age group, and slid to 40 percent for those ages 60 to 64. It is fair to say that for those over 50 who are not eligible for Medicare, coverage is widely available, but often not at the standard prices quoted by health insurance companies.

WHERE TO LOOK, WHAT TO ASK

The best website we found in searching for health insurance policy information and quotes was ehealthinsurance.com. Links to hundreds of health insurance companies are available at the America's Health Insurance Plans website at ahip.org. The "consumer information" icon takes you to consumer guides on many health topics and links to dozens of health insurance companies. You can find insurance agents at the Association of Health Insurance Advisors website at www.ahia.net, or through the National Association of Health Underwriters website at www.nahu.org.

Here is a checklist of items to consider in researching and comparing health insurance policies:

Health Insurance Policy Checklist			
Provision	Policy A	Policy B	Policy C
Name of plan			
Financial rating of company			
Monthly premium			
Deductibles			
Copayments			
Coinsurance			
Out-of-network charge			
Out-of-pocket annual limit			
Doctor visit			
Prescriptions			
Mental health			
Emergency room			
Outpatient surgery			
Hospitalization			
Annual benefit maximum			
Lifetime maximum			

THE FINE PRINT MATTERS

When you are considering policies, look up the specific provisions online, or ask for a booklet with all the details. Examine the plan with your own health care usage in mind. It's not easy reading, but a little work can save lots of money and major hassles later on. Make sure you get a "guaranteed renewable" policy. The company can raise your premiums but cannot cancel the policy as long as you pay the premium. Verify that there is a "free look" clause. With most companies, you have at least 10 days to examine the plan after you receive the policy. If you are dissatisfied, you can return it for a premium refund. If all the individual plans look too expensive, you have another option: a high deductible plan with a Health Savings Account.

HEALTH SAVINGS ACCOUNTS

We examine Health Savings Accounts (HSA) separately because they are covered by their own set of policy limits and tax regulations. Legislation authorizing these plans was signed into law by President Bush in December 2003. Under an HSA, a consumer purchases a special health insurance policy called a "high deductible health plan" (HDHP). Most of these plans also have a very high annual out-of-pocket limit. The policyholder can set aside pretax dollars in a Health Savings Account from which funds are used to pay medical bills. Because the consumer takes on much more of the financial burden of health care, premiums for these policies tend to be more affordable than for traditional health insurance plans. Between the low cost of an HDHP and the considerable tax advantages of the HSA, this combination may be the answer for some Boomers trying to plug the gap until the Medicare cavalry arrives.

HSA advocates contend that because these policies put consumers on the hook for more of their medical expenditures, they will be more aggressive when shopping for health care services. Putting to work the American penchant for sniffing out bargains, they say, will make the marketplace more efficient and lead to lower health care costs. Critics see these plans as yet another way for businesses and insurance companies to shift the burden of rapidly rising health care costs onto individuals. They also worry that people with HSAs will delay seeking medical care because they will have to pay for it out of pocket.

Who Can Have an HSA?

- Anyone under age 65 who buys a qualified high deductible policy can open an HSA.
- You cannot be covered by another health insurance policy that isn't a qualified HDHP, but you can still have other disability, dental, vision, and long-term care insurance policies.
- Policies can be obtained by individuals or businesses. Both employers and employees can make tax-deductible contributions to HSAs.
- There are no income limits on who can open an HSA or take advantage of the tax benefits.

High Deductible Health Plans: The Mechanics

- As the name implies, HDHPs have high deductibles, at least $1,100 per year for individual policies in 2007, and $2,200 for family policies. The deductibles are generally higher than these legal minimums.
- Total out-of-pocket expenses, including deductibles, copayments, and coinsurance, cannot exceed $5,500 for individuals or $11,000 for family coverage in 2007. The out-of-pocket limit does not include policy premiums.
- When you open an HSA, you typically receive a checkbook or debit card, which you can use to pay for qualified medical expenses.

- You do not have to submit medical receipts to a plan administrator, but keep accurate records in the event of a tax audit.

The Tax-Break Carrot

A new HSA tax break took effect in 2007 that makes the plans even more attractive. Under the original law, tax-deductible contributions to HSAs could not exceed the amount of the policy deductible. As of 2007, a new law allows tax-deductible contributions of $2,850 for single coverage and $5,650 for family coverage, even if the policy deductible is lower. Individuals age 55 and older can *each* make additional "catch-up" contributions:

- $800 in 2007
- $900 in 2008
- $1,000 in 2009 and beyond

Example. A fifty-five-year-old married couple in the 25 percent federal tax bracket, making the maximum contributions, would cut their tax bill by $1,812.50 in 2007. Here is how:

- Maximum HSA contribution: $5,650
- Two "catch-up" contributions: $1,600
- Total deductible contributions: $7,250
- Total tax savings: $7,250 × .25 = $1,812.50

Many states also allow for tax deductions of HSA contributions.

Rules of the Road

- HSA accounts can be established at banks, credit unions, and other financial institutions. Check several plans to compare account fees.

- Funds can be placed in interest-bearing accounts or growth-oriented mutual funds.
- Money can be withdrawn tax-free to pay for qualified medical expenses. IRS Publication 502 lists "qualified expenses."
- Account balances can be rolled over from year to year.
- If you change medical coverage out of an HDHP, you can still use your HSA to pay for medical expenses, but you can no longer contribute to the plan.
- Long-term care insurance policies can be purchased with HSA funds.
- Medicare recipients cannot open or contribute to an HSA, but can use an existing account to pay for medical expenses tax-free.
- You can use your HSA to pay Medicare premiums, deductibles, copays, and coinsurance.
- Prior to age 65, funds used for nonmedical purposes are subject to income tax and a 10 percent penalty.
- After age 65, funds used for nonmedical expenses are subject to tax, but no penalty.

Extra Tax Savings

If you are self-employed, you may be able to deduct the full cost of health insurance you purchase for yourself, your spouse, and your dependents. This applies to both HSAs and individual health insurance policies. You can deduct health insurance premiums up to the amount of net profit you report on Schedule C. You can only take the deduction for premiums paid in months when you were not eligible to participate in a group health insurance plan through your employer or your spouse's employer. Form 1040 instructions include a worksheet to calculate the health care premium deduction.

HDHPs: Lifting the Hood

Below is an example of a high deductible health plan from www.ehealthinsurance.com. It is for a hypothetical couple in San Diego, California. The man is age 62, the woman age 60. The plan was available as of April 15, 2007.

Policy Applicants	62-year-old man, 60-year-woman from San Diego, California
Name of Plan	Aetna Preventive and Hospital Care 3000 (HSA compatible)
Type	PPO
Financial Rating	A (Excellent)
Monthly Premium	$449.00
Deductible	Family: $6000
Coinsurance	20% after deductible
Out-of-Pocket	Family: $10000 (includes deductible)
Doctor Visit	Not covered, except physical every 24 months with $35 copay
Prescriptions	Not covered, discount card available
ER	$100 copay, waived if admitted, plus 20% coinsurance after deductible
Outpatient Surgery	20% coinsurance after deductible
Hospitalization	20% coinsurance after deductible
Lifetime Maximum	$5 million

Plan Analysis

As you would expect with a high deductible health plan, the premium is relatively low and the coverage is scant. It illustrates why some people refer to HDHPs as "catastrophic insurance." The deductible is $6,000, after which coinsurance of 20 percent kicks in until the out-of-pocket maximum of $10,000 is reached. This is in addition to the $5,388 in premiums. Maximum HSA contributions for this couple would save $1,812 in taxes, and would also build up a substantial war chest for handling medical costs in a bad year. If either spouse has a chronic medical condition requiring frequent treatment and a steady need for medications, this is not the right policy. Instead, they should investigate a traditional policy with lower deductibles. But if they are generally healthy, and if out-of-pocket medical needs are in the $1,000 to $3,000 range, the couple's annual health care bill would be about $6,500 to $8,500, including insurance premiums. The tax break would lower the true cost. In three years, the husband becomes eligible for Medicare, and the wife can take out a lower-cost policy until she reaches the Medicare threshold.

HSA Policy Predicament

The HDHP-HSA combo has the potential to be very attractive to healthy young people who would enjoy substantial savings through lower premiums. Affluent Americans, who tend to have better than average health, may be drawn to HSAs for the tax advantages. But what happens if large numbers of healthy people abandon traditional health insurance plans? Overall, the remaining pool of consumers would be less healthy, and their medical costs would no longer be shared by those who've migrated to the promised land of HSAs. That could mean even higher insurance premiums for the less healthy (and less wealthy) who are stuck behind in traditional plans. The concept takes us further away from a collective responsibility for the basic need for health care, and toward a market-driven attitude that says, "I'm all set, and buddy, you're on your own."

MAKING A HEALTHY CHANGE

With so much focus on health insurance, we don't want to skip over the most important advice of all: doing all we can to preserve our health and avoid using our medical insurance. It's pretty easy to take good health for granted as the years slip by. Sometimes it takes a wake-up call to make us change. That's just what happened to David and Lynne Blake as they started a vacation in December 2004. "Right after we arrived in Florida I had an episode," says Lynne. "My heart was racing and I was having atrial fibrillation. The ambulance came and took me to Key West Medical Center. It took them six or seven hours to get my heart back in proper rhythm. They kept me in ICU for two days. I was let out on Christmas and, of course, was scared half to death by the episode."

At around the same time, David started having chest pains. The couple, early retirees in their late fifties, knew they had to do something. Lynne remembers that her cardiologist in Florida sat them both down for a stern discussion about health. "He said, 'You are both overweight, you are having too good a time. You're retired and if you want to live longer to enjoy your retirement, you need to do something about it.' He said, 'I want you to go out and buy the South Beach diet book today, and go on the diet tomorrow,' and we did."

They made a major change in diet, cutting back on potatoes, rolls, junk food, and fats. They started eating more vegetables, soups, and salads. They learned to use spices to make the food tastier. At first, shopping and preparing meals took much longer than usual as they adjusted to the new regimen. They combined the better diet with more exercise, walking an hour a day. Back home on Cape Cod, they continued to build their new habits and started shedding pounds. Lynne lost 35 pounds and David dropped 50.

"Now I've got a little bounce in my step," says David. "Carrying around an extra 40 or 50 pounds, it made quite a difference. I do a lot of carpentry work, up and down ladders, and losing the weight has made a huge difference."

"I used to get out of breath," recalls Lynne. "We just moved into this house recently and I never had a house with two floors. I can run up and down the stairs all day long and not even think about it. That would have been a problem before. I would have been dragging myself up and down just carrying that extra weight around. I used to have back trouble and that seems to be pretty much gone. I have a lot more energy and can do more."

Seven months after their scare in Florida, David and Lynne were optimistic about staying on the road to better health. "We are staying a lot more active," says David. "We both enjoy boating and doing stuff together. We like to dig shellfish. We lobster, and we hope to be able to keep doing that for many years. I don't think it's ever too late. So much of what you do is really habit. Once you change your habits a little bit and start to lose a little weight and feel more physically fit, you feel so much better. It's a great thing."

"I think anybody can do this at any time," says Lynne. "And it's certainly going to make a difference."

13

HEALTH CARE FOR THE LONG HAUL

Medicare is one of America's great success stories. Nearly 44 million Americans get health coverage through Medicare. Most are age 65 and older; some 7 million people with permanent disabilities who are under age 65 are also covered. Prior to its passage in 1965, about half of all seniors lacked medical insurance; today, virtually all older Americans have health insurance under Medicare. The program pays for many vital health care services, including hospitalizations, physician services, and a new prescription drug benefit. Medicare does not cover long-term nursing home care. Later in this chapter, we will delve into long-term care insurance.

MEDICARE OVERVIEW

Medicare is not socialized medicine. It is a giant health insurance operation that pays for services provided by the private sector health care industry. Because of its scale and because it has no highly paid executives or lobbyists, no marketing budgets, and makes no profit, it is run more efficiently than private health insurance. Administrative costs take up 2 percent of the Medicare budget compared to a health insurance industry average of about 10 percent.

In 2006, Medicare benefit payments totaled $374 billion, accounting for 13 percent of federal spending. Medicare is financed by the payroll tax, general revenues, and premiums paid by beneficiaries. The portion of the payroll tax dedicated to Medicare totals 2.9 percent, split evenly between workers and employers. Medicare's financial stability will be under strain as millions of Boomers qualify for coverage starting in 2011.

According to the Kaiser Family Foundation, if current trends continue, Medicare expenditures as a share of GDP are projected to rise from 3.1 percent in 2007 to 7.3 percent in 2035. Eventually, a new funding plan will be needed to shore up Medicare. A possible sign of things to come occurred in 2007 when, for the first time, high-income Medicare participants were charged higher premiums for part of their coverage.

As Boomers look to the future, Medicare is a central piece of the life-planning puzzle. Boomers who are assisting parents with medical issues also need to know at least the fundamentals of Medicare. Vast amounts of information on Medicare are available online, so we will not go deep into the intricacies of the coverage. However, we think a general overview of the benefits is useful, along with some tips on avoiding pitfalls that could cost you money.

Who Qualifies

You are eligible for Medicare if you meet the following criteria:

- You are a U.S. citizen or have been a permanent legal resident for five continuous years, and you are 65 years or older.

You also qualify if any of the following apply:

- You are under 65, disabled, and have been receiving Social Security Disability Insurance (SSDI) for at least 24 months.
- You get continuing dialysis for permanent kidney failure or need a kidney transplant.
- You have Amyotrophic Lateral Sclerosis (ALS—Lou Gehrig's disease).

Enrollment

Although full retirement age for Social Security is rising, 65 remains as the starting date for Medicare eligibility. If you are already getting Social Security when you turn 65, you will automatically get both Medicare Part A and Part B on the first day of the month in which you turn 65. A red, white, and blue Medicare card will be mailed to you about three months before your birthday. You do not have to be retired to enroll in Medicare.

If you are not getting Social Security when you turn 65, go to your local Social Security office to enroll in Medicare three months before your 65th birthday. You have seven months to enroll in Medicare without incurring a penalty, starting three months before the month you turn 65. The penalty is meant to encourage you to sign up and start paying premiums. In most cases, you can avoid the penalty if you, or your spouse, are still working and receiving group insurance coverage. Call 1-800-772-1213 for the address of your local Social Security office.

MEDICARE BENEFITS

Medicare consists of four parts, each covering different health care needs:

1. Part A, also known as the *Hospital Insurance* program, covers inpatient hospital services and skilled nursing facilities. It also covers home health care and hospice care.
2. Part B, the *Medical Insurance* program, helps cover doctors' services, many medical tests, and outpatient care. You have your choice of doctors.
3. Part C, also known as the *Medicare Advantage* program, allows beneficiaries to enroll in a private insurance plan, such as an HMO. Generally, you must see doctors in the plan.
4. Part D is the *Prescription Drug* program started in 2006.

Many participants also have *supplemental plans* to fill gaps in Medicare coverage. These plans may be "Medigap" policies sold by private insurers, or insurance provided by current or former employers.

All dollar amounts in the following descriptions are for 2007 rates. All premiums and deductibles in Medicare are adjusted each year for inflation. Coinsurance rises as the underlying charges go up.

PART A

Most Medicare recipients do not pay for Part A coverage; you bought this coverage with a lifetime of payroll taxes. You are eligible for free Part A coverage if you paid into Social Security for at least 10 years, or you are eligible to receive Social Security benefits on your spouse's earnings. If you (or your spouse) do not have enough years of credited work but do meet the age and residency requirements, you can purchase Medicare Part A for a monthly premium of up to $410.00.

Hospital Coverage

The principal benefit of Part A is hospital insurance. It pays for a semiprivate room, meals, general nursing, and other hospital services and supplies. This includes inpatient care you get in critical access hospitals and mental health care. This doesn't include private-duty nursing or a television or telephone in your room. It also does not include a private room, unless medically necessary.

Part A has a $992 deductible for the first 60 days in a hospital, called a "benefit period." If you have a second hospital stay that starts more than 60 days after the first benefit period ends, you must pay another $992 deductible. This cycle can continue throughout the year, resulting in multiple deductible payments. If you return to the hospital less than 60 days after being discharged, you are in the same benefit period and do not have to pay an additional deductible.

If you are hospitalized for more than 60 days in one benefit period, coinsurance kicks in and you have to pay:

Days 61 to 90	$248 per day
Days 91 to 150	$496 per day
After 150 days	$496 per day for 60 lifetime reserve days

Skilled Nursing Facility Care

If you are recovering from an illness or injury that required at least a three-day inpatient hospital stay, Part A pays for treatment in a skilled nursing facility. You are covered for a semiprivate room, meals, skilled nursing and rehabilitative services, and other services and supplies for up to 100 days in a benefit period.

Coverage for a skilled nursing facility:

Days 1 to 20	no coinsurance
Days 21 to 100	$124 per day coinsurance
After 100 days	no coverage

Home Health Care Services

If your doctor decides that you need medical care at home, Medicare will cover the costs with no deductible or coinsurance. To qualify, the services must be limited to reasonable and necessary part-time or intermittent care for the following:

- Skilled nursing care
- Physical therapy
- Speech-language therapy
- Occupational therapy

The patient must be homebound, or normally unable to leave home unassisted. The home health agency providing care must be Medicare-certified. Coverage also includes durable medical equipment such as wheelchairs, hospital beds, oxygen, walkers, and medical supplies for use at home. A 20 percent coinsurance applies for Medicare-approved durable medical equipment.

Hospice

For people with a terminal illness (less than six months to live), Part A covers hospice care. Coverage includes drugs for symptom control and pain relief, and medical and support services from a Medicare-approved hospice. Hospice care is usually given in the home (or a nursing facility if that is where the patient lives). Medicare also covers some short-term hospital and inpatient respite care (care given to a hospice patient so that the usual caregiver can rest).

You have a copayment of up to $5 for outpatient prescription drugs, and five percent of the Medicare-approved amount for inpatient respite care.

PART B

Part B, which pays for doctor bills and outpatient services, is funded by general federal revenues and beneficiary premiums. The standard monthly premium in 2007 is $93.50 per month. Starting in 2007, Medicare beneficiaries who have annual incomes over $80,000 for singles and $160,000 for couples pay a higher Part B premium (see details on the following page).

Patients have an annual Part B deductible of $131 before Medicare pays any claims. Many medical services under Part B, including doctor visits, have 20 percent coinsurance. Coinsurance of 50 percent is charged for outpatient mental health services.

Part B also covers a number of preventive medical tests including mammograms, Pap smears, colon cancer screening, prostate screening, and diabetes testing. In most cases, coinsurance applies.

Example: You go into the hospital for a hip replacement. Medicare Part A pays the hospital bill. Part B pays fees for the surgeon and anesthetist. If you need to recover in a skilled nursing facility, Part A picks up the cost. The patient would have to pay a hospital deductible of $992, plus 20 percent coinsurance for the doctors (and possibly the $131 Part B annual deductible). The skilled nursing facility would be covered in full for up to 20 days.

Many of these charges, or gaps in coverage, can be covered through additional insurance called Medigap, which we will outline later. Part B premiums are deducted automatically from Social Security payments. A common complaint is that much of the annual cost-of-living increase in Social Security is eaten up by faster rising Medicare premiums.

Monthly Premiums

Here comes IRMA, or the "income-related Medicare adjustment." Congress approved a progressive premium structure for Part B, raising rates for high-income Medicare recipients. The new rates took effect in 2007, and will be phased in over three years. It's the first time income benchmarks have been used to have participants pay above the standard rate for coverage. Here is how the change affected 2007 rates:

| If your yearly income is . . . | | You pay |
Individual	Joint Return	(per person)
$80,000 or less	$160,000 or less	$93.50 (standard premium)
$80,001–$100,000	$160,001–$200,000	$105.80
$100,001–$150,000	$200,001–$300,000	$124.40
$150,001–$200,000	$300,001–$400,000	$142.90
Above $200,000	Above $400,000	$161.40

The rate is based on income from two years prior, meaning 2007 rates are determined by 2005 income.

The full increase takes effect over three years, with one-third of the hike being applied per year. About four percent of Medicare Part B participants are paying the price for IRMA. Income limits are indexed for inflation.

Example: If you file a single tax return and make between $80,000 and $100,000 per year, you pay a monthly premium of $105.80, or $12.30 more than the standard rate. If the full impact of IRMA were in effect, you would pay about $37.00 over the base premium, or 40 percent more than the standard rate.

If your income has gone down since 2005, you can contact Social Security and appeal for a lower premium. Among the reasons allowed for an adjustment:

- You have married, divorced, or your spouse died.
- You or your spouse have stopped working or reduced your work hours.

Penalty Flag

If you are age 65 and automatically enrolled in Medicare, you will be signed up for both Parts A and B. But Part B is optional; you can decline the coverage. However, if you don't sign up for Part B when it is first available, you may end up paying a penalty if you opt for the coverage later on. If you initially pass on the coverage but decide to enroll at a later date, the cost of Part B goes up 10 percent for each full 12-month period that you could have had Part B but didn't sign up for it. The penalty would apply for as long as you have Part B.

The penalty does not apply if you, or your spouse, were still working and you were covered under a group health plan from an employer or union. As long as you sign up for Part B within eight months of the end of that group coverage, you are not penalized. (The eight-month clock starts ticking on the first of the month in which coverage ends.) The idea of the penalty is to encourage people to sign up and pay for Part B even if they are healthy at age 65. Insurance doesn't work if people can delay signing up until they get sick and are about to run up big bills.

PART C—MEDICARE ADVANTAGE

The Medicare Advantage program allows beneficiaries to enroll in a private plan, such as a health maintenance organization (HMO), preferred provider organization (PPO), or private fee-for-service (PFFS) plan. These plans receive payments from Medicare to provide services.

When you join a Medicare Advantage Plan, you are still in Medicare. You must pay your monthly Part B premium. In addition, you generally pay a monthly premium to your Medicare Advantage Plan for extra benefits such as prescription coverage. You may be able to choose from among dozens of plans, each with its own premiums, coverage, and copayments. Through the Medicare website at www.medicare.gov, you can find Medicare Advantage Plans available by zip code. As of January 2007, 8.3 million people had Medicare Advantage Plans, nearly one in five Medicare participants.

About Medicare Advantage Plans

- Medicare estimates that the average participant saves about $100 per month in the total cost of premiums and other payments compared with a traditional Medicare plan.

- You cannot combine a Medigap policy with the Medicare Advantage Plan.
- The plans provide all of your Part A (hospital) and Part B (medical) coverage and must cover medically necessary services.
- They often have networks, which means you may have to see doctors who belong to the plan or go to certain hospitals to get covered services.
- Many plans require referrals to see specialists.
- Most include prescription drug coverage.

Medicare Advantage Plans may also offer supplemental benefits for which they can charge an additional premium. Examples of these benefits include vision, hearing, preventive dental care, podiatry, and chiropractic services. If you want to keep seeing your current doctors, call them before joining to make sure they are in the HMO network and are taking new HMO patients.

PART D—PRESCRIPTION COVERAGE

Medicare Part D is the prescription drug program that began with great fanfare and controversy in 2006. Private insurers operating under Medicare rules sell coverage either as stand-alone prescription drug plans or through Medicare Advantage Plans. Beneficiaries in most states have a choice of at least 50 stand-alone plans and multiple Medicare Advantage drug plans.

Part D plans are required to offer either a "standard benefit" as defined by law, or an alternative of equivalent value. Plans can also offer coverage with enhanced benefits. In 2007, the average annual premium for a standard plan was $328. Plans may include a monthly premium, annual deductible, and prescription copayments. Your total cost depends considerably on prescription usage. Part D is also subsidized with additional payments from Medicare.

Falling Through the Donut Hole

One big drawback in Part D is the infamous "donut hole." This is the gap in coverage between $2,400 and $5,451 in total drug spending for the year. It is a $3,051 chasm in which the consumer must pay 100 percent of prescription bills. Above that limit, insurance covers most of the rest of the year's prescription costs, but only after the beneficiary has taken a beating. Nevertheless, many Medicare participants are paying lower prescription bills under this new coverage.

Finding Prescription Coverage

The Medicare website (www.medicare.gov) has a Medicare Prescription Drug Plan Finder that can help you learn about plans in your area by accessing a directory of all Medicare plans with drug coverage in your state. You can click on a plan name for up-to-date detailed cost and coverage information, including whether or not the plan covers the drugs you take. You can make comparisons by checking out several plans. Factors to consider include the following:

- Drug coverage; does the plan cover the medications you need?
- Cost; consider premiums, deductibles, copayments.
- Convenience; are the plans' retail outlets near where you live or shop?

Every year between November 15 and December 31, you can switch to a different Medicare drug plan if your needs change. If you have limited income and resources, you may qualify for extra help in paying for Medicare drug plan costs. You can apply or get more information by calling Social Security at 1-800-772-1213.

Penalty Flag

Here is another example of where you can be penalized if you don't sign up for coverage as soon as you can. If you do not purchase prescription drug coverage during your initial enrollment period but decide to enroll later, you may be penalized every month for as long as you keep the coverage. To estimate the penalty, take one percent of the national average monthly premium for the year you join, and multiply it by the number of full months you were eligible to join a Medicare drug plan but didn't. This estimated penalty amount is added each month to your drug plan premium for as long as you have a plan.

Example: Edward delays joining a prescription drug plan for 15 months after being eligible. He finally joins in late 2007. The national average Part D monthly premium in 2007 is $27.35. One percent of that is 27 cents. Multiply .27 by the 15-month delay and his monthly penalty will be $4.05 for the rest of the time he is in the plan. This is done to encourage healthy people to join the drug plan early, and to penalize those who may delay getting coverage until their prescription bills start to mount.

People who do not enroll in Part D when first eligible can avoid the penalty if they already had drug coverage from an employer or union health plan. That coverage must be "creditable," which means it is as good as or better than Medicare's drug coverage. Employers or unions must provide information on whether their plans meet the creditable standard. The penalty is waived if the individual signs up for Part D within 63 days of the ending of their coverage in a creditable plan.

MEDIGAP—MEDICARE SUPPLEMENT INSURANCE

As we have seen, Medicare provides significant health care coverage, but also leaves many expensive gaps such as the $992 hospitalization deductible and 20 percent coinsurance for doctors' bills. Medigap insurance can fill some or most of those holes, depending on the policy you buy. For those who use Medicare Part A and Part B, Medigap plans can lower your out-of-pocket costs and provide additional insurance. The plans are offered by private insurers, which can sell only "standardized" Medigap policies. There are 12 policies designated "A" through "L." Each has a specific set of benefits, with higher prices for more comprehensive coverage. Companies can set their own prices, but, by law, all policies with the same letter have the same benefits, making it easier to comparison shop. These are individual plans. For a married couple, each spouse must purchase separate coverage.

After selecting the plan you want, shop around for the best price available in your area. But check the financial rating of the insurance company before buying a policy. Look for an A.M. Best rating of B+ (very good) or better (www.ambest.com). The Medicare Rights Center has an excellent chart on its website illustrating the different Medigap plans and their coverage (www.medicarerights.org.). The Medicare website (www.medicare.gov.) lets you search for Medigap policies by zip code. Go to the home page and scroll down to "Compare Health Plans and Medigap Policies in Your Area."

Medigap Plan Features

With 12 policies and about a dozen different areas of coverage, it takes a bit of study to pick your plan. However, you can quickly sort through some of the options. Plans H, I, and J are no longer open to new applicants. They include limited prescription coverage, but Medicare wants people to sign up for Part D, so these plans are not on the menu for Boomers.

Plans K and L, available since 2005, are low premium policies that provide modest insurance. They both cover hospital coinsurance for days 61 to 90 ($248) and days 91 to 150 ($496) in the hospital. They also include payment in full for 365 additional lifetime days in the hospital. In addition, they have partial coverage for the $992 hospital deductible and 20 percent coinsurance under Part B. Plan K has an annual out-of-pocket maximum of $4,000. Plan L has a $2,000 maximum. Both policies pay 100 percent of Part A and Part B coinsurance after annual maximums have been spent.

Of the remaining seven plans, A through G, many of the features overlap, but each has at least one distinctive benefit or shortcoming. All seven cover hospital coinsurance for days 61 to 150, and payment in full for 365 additional lifetime days. They all pick up coinsurance for Part B such as doctors' services, laboratory and X-ray services, durable medical equipment, and hospital outpatient services. They all pay for the first three pints of blood needed in the hospital.

Plan A, however, does not cover the $992 hospital stay deductible, while plans B through G do pick up that cost. Plans C through G cover $124 per day for days 21 to 100 of skilled care in a nursing home, as well as limited coverage for emergency care when traveling overseas; plans A and B do not have those features. Plans C and F are the most comprehensive and most popular. They also pick up the annual Part B deductible of $131.

This gives you a sense of the choices involved. Spend 15 minutes with the Medicare Rights Center Medigap chart and you'll have a good feel for how to make your selection. Then go to the Medicare website to find which companies offer the plan you want in your area. You will have to contact the companies directly for pricing information. Your state insurance department may also have helpful information.

Insurers can choose which plans they want to offer, but all policies are identical by letter. For example, a Plan C offered by one company in Texas is the same as a Plan C offered by another insurer in Pennsylvania. Of course, there have to be some exceptions. If you live in Massachusetts, Minnesota, or Wisconsin, different types of standardized Medigap policies are sold in your state.

Medigap Prices

Since the Medigap policies all have the same coverage, the major area of difference is in pricing. Companies price these policies in three ways:

Community rated: The same monthly premium is charged to everyone who has the Medigap policy, regardless of age. Premiums may go up because of inflation. Younger policyholders tend to subsidize older people with this system, but then those younger folks hope to be older themselves someday.

Issue-age rated: The premium is based on your age when you buy (are "issued") the Medigap policy. Premiums are lower for younger buyers. Premiums may go up because of inflation. If you buy a policy at 65 and live a long time, this probably works out best.

Attained-age rated: The premium is based on your current age (the age you have "attained") so your premium goes up over time. Premiums for these Medigap policies are low for younger buyers, but can eventually become the most expensive. Premiums may also go up because of inflation.

Insurance companies may offer discounts to females, nonsmokers, and/or married people.

Plan F is the most comprehensive Medigap plan, so we checked prices for a sixty-five-year-old man signing up for Medigap insurance as soon as he is eligible. Here were the premiums in four cities in March 2007:

Seattle, WA	$144.50/mo.	$1,734/yr.
Albuquerque, NM	$117.20/mo.	$1,406/yr.
Indianapolis, IN	$128.40/mo.	$1,541/yr.
New York, NY	$220.75/mo.	$2,649/yr.

These were all community-rated policies, meaning all policyholders pay the same regardless of age. Other policies are priced differently, some with lower starting premiums that rise over time. You have to work the phone, sharpen your pencil, and get out the calculator to determine the best deal for you.

Open Enrollment

The best time to buy a Medigap policy is during your Medigap "open enrollment period." That's a six-month window that begins on the first day of the month in which you and your spouse are both:

- Age 65 or older
- Enrolled in Medicare Part B

Once your six-month Medigap open enrollment period starts, it can't be changed. During this period, an insurance company cannot deny you Medigap coverage or charge you more for a policy because of health problems. If you are still covered by an employer health plan at age 65 and have not signed up for Part B, you are not yet into your open enrollment period. Once you get a Medigap policy it is guaranteed renewable each year, unless you fail to pay premiums, you aren't truthful about something under the Medigap policy, or the company goes bankrupt.

Penalty Flag

If you apply for a Medigap policy after your open enrollment period has ended, the insurance company is allowed to consider your medical history in deciding whether to sell you a policy and how much to charge. The only way to guarantee that you get a Medigap policy at the standard rate is to buy it during a qualified enrollment period. Some states have additional protections.

BUDGETING FOR HEALTH CARE

Even with all the health insurance coverage we have been describing, medical expenses for older Americans are taking an ever-larger chunk out of the household budget. Financial advisors are increasingly incorporating health care planning into retirement scenarios, and the numbers will mean a change of plans for some Boomers. Probably a few less Winnebagos will hit the road and a few less cups of cappuccino will be served at sidewalk cafés in Paris.

The Kaiser Family Foundation reports that "Medicare has relatively high cost-sharing requirements and covers less than half (45 percent) of beneficiaries' total costs." Medicare does not pay for routine dental care and dentures, routine vision care or eyeglasses, or hearing exams and hearing aids. "Although many beneficiaries have supplemental insurance to help cover these expenses, they may still face significant out-of-pocket costs to meet their medical and long-term care needs," according to the Kaiser study.

Here is a rundown of typical health care costs for a well-insured sixty-five-year-old man who lives in Boston and is in good health. He is covered by Medicare Parts A and B, the Part D prescription drug plan, and has a good Medigap policy. We'll assume he takes a daily dose of Lipitor (20 mg) to keep cholesterol under control. He wears glasses and sees the dentist twice a year.

Medical Cost	Monthly	Annual
Medicare Part B premium	$93.50	$1122.00
Part D prescription premium	$26.30	$315.60
Part D prescription copay	$28.00	$336.00
Medigap premium	$159.00	$1908.00
Eye exam	$10.42	$125.00
New glasses	$14.58	$175.00
Dental visits (2)	$25.00	$300.00
Over-the-counter medications	$15.00	$180.00
Totals	$371.80	$4461.60

So, our sixty-five-year-old had out-of-pocket medical costs of $4,461 for the year. And this is for a healthy guy who had a pretty good year. Yes, he had to buy glasses, which he doesn't do every year. But he had just routine checkups at the dentist, which is not always the case. There will definitely be worse years ahead. Remember this is just one person. All of the insurance coverage is for individuals. You can double this figure for a couple, to just under $9,000. Over a 25-year retirement, that would total $225,000, not counting inflation, and not counting a possible costly decline in health. For anyone who thinks his or her medical bills will go way down once they make it to the Medicare safe zone, these numbers are a chilling wake-up call.

While this package of Medicare-related insurance coverage provides a sturdy health care safety net, the Kaiser report, mentioned earlier, reminds us of one glaring lack of coverage: "Medicare does not pay for custodial long-term care services either at home or in an institution, such as a nursing home or assisted living facility." To meet the ravaging costs of nursing home care, either we are on our own or we spend down our resources to poverty level and go on Medicaid. Or, we can purchase long-term care insurance.

LONG-TERM CARE

One of the great fears of old age is ending up warehoused in a nursing home, unable to take care of our own daily needs, while a lifetime of savings goes down the drain.

It does happen. However, there are ways to reduce the likelihood of that occurring, and to manage the financial impact if it does. Understanding the risk is a good start. Some 83 percent of long-term care takes place in the home or the community, with just 17 percent provided by nursing homes, according to a Georgetown University study. For Boomers, discussion of long-term care has a dual purpose. First, we may have to confront these issues with our parents. Second, it's wise to get an early start on our own long-term care planning.

With longer life expectancies, Boomers can expand the continuum of elder care and create new models for aging outside of nursing homes. "I think there will be a big movement toward home care," says financial planner Dee Lee of Harvard, Massachusetts. "Many councils on aging are getting more active in helping people to stay in their homes." Meals on wheels, homemaker services, drop-by programs, and telephone check-in networks can be employed.

Family members and friends can provide elder care. Residents in cohousing can take care of each other. Home health care services and adult day care facilities can be expanded. The number of assisted living and continuing care communities is growing, allowing older people to live more independently. No doubt, many new businesses will be started to assist an aging population with services that are less costly and less restrictive than traditional nursing homes. We should not stand by hoping for answers from an overburdened federal government; solutions will have to come from the grass roots.

Boomers can lead by example through volunteer work. Healthy Boomers in their sixties can volunteer to help older people remain in their homes by doing errands and assisting with household chores, like bill paying. Dee Lee cites an example of an elderly woman who paid a charitable solicitation every month because she thought it was a bill. "Volunteers can go through the bills and say, 'This is a bill, and this is a charitable request.' It can be a big help in maintaining independence," says Lee. Once these programs are up and running, Boomers can benefit when they are in their eighties.

Back in their twenties, many Boomers broke down social barriers and shocked their parents by living together before getting married. Dee Lee says we are seeing a new twist on that arrangement among older people today. "More older men and women are living together to take care of each other," she says. "But they are not tying the knot legally or financially, so they won't be responsible if their partner goes into a nursing home." In redefining aging, Boomers will create a new prototype of elder care. But despite the alternatives, many will need the intensive level of care provided by a nursing home.

ACTIVITIES OF DAILY LIVING—ADL

People who enter nursing homes are usually experiencing some combination of chronic physical and/or mental impairments. They are unable to perform some of the simple daily tasks that most of us take for granted. These tasks have a clinical name, "activities of daily living," or ADL, and they include the following:

- Eating
- Dressing
- Bathing
- Toileting (using the bathroom)
- Transferring (moving back and forth from a bed to a chair)
- Continence

Some families assume the loving commitment of caring for elders who can no longer perform some of these activities of daily living. But not everyone can take that on. For some, nursing home care may become the only alternative. During nursing home stays, Medicare remains in effect for medical treatment. Medicare coupled with most Medigap policies pays for up to 100 days in a nursing home, if the nursing home admission is preceded by a hospital stay of at least three days.

FINANCING LONG-TERM CARE

Three primary alternatives are available to pay for long-term care. One option is to self-insure. An individual or family with enough wealth to pay for home-based or nursing home care may choose to pay for services with their own resources. One approach is to establish a special investment fund to build up reserves for long-term care, if the need arises. If the care isn't necessary, the money stays in the family.

A second option is to rely on Medicaid. As noted, Medicare does not pay for long-term nursing home care, but Medicaid covers those costs for people with minimal assets. For elders who have no savings, this is clearly the way to go. They have the least to lose before Medicaid takes over. Some people start paying for their own care when they enter a nursing home, and then spend down their assets to the poverty limit, at which point Medicaid starts paying the bills. Others transfer assets to family members in order to qualify for Medicaid, but federal law says that any funds transferred within five years of entering a nursing home will still be counted as assets in determining Medicaid eligibility. This "look-back" period has been lengthened several times over the years as more families employed this strategy, and Congress may extend it again in the future. Seek qualified legal advice to handle such a property transfer.

If you have assets that you would like to pass on, but cannot afford to comfortably self-insure against nursing home expenses, long-term care insurance may be the answer. Long-term care insurance policies pay for care up to a daily dollar limit for a specified period. The higher the dollar limit and the longer the coverage period, the more expensive the policy will be.

LONG-TERM CARE POLICY FEATURES

Better policies cover long-term care in a variety of settings, including the home, adult day care, assisted living, and a nursing home. This gives you control over where and how you receive care. A typical policy might contain the following features:

- Nursing home benefit $150/day
- Home care benefit $125/day
- Policy benefit period   3 years
- Waiting period   90 days
- Inflation protection   5 percent compounded

Here is a provision from a long-term care insurance policy on what must happen for benefits to be paid:

> "Either 1) You need substantial assistance (i.e., "hands-on" or "standby") with at least two of six activities of daily living (bathing, dressing, eating, toileting, transferring, and continence) for a period of at least 90 days due to a loss of functional capacity; or 2) you require substantial supervision to protect yourself from threats to health and safety due to severe cognitive impairment. A licensed health care practitioner (e.g., your doctor) must certify that you have met one of the above requirements and must prescribe a plan of care."

How Much Coverage

Where you live can determine how much coverage to buy. Daily nursing home rates vary considerably across the country. Here is a sampling:

Location	Daily Rate	Annual Cost
Shreveport, LA	$104	$37,960
Des Moines, IA	$142	$51,830
Lexington, KY	$158	$57,670
Colorado Springs, CO	$165	$60,225
New York, NY	$333	$121,545

Source: "The MetLife Market Survey of Nursing Home and Home Care Costs," The MetLife Mature Market Institute, September 2006

In 2006, the national average cost of a semiprivate room in a nursing home was $66,795 a year with an average stay of 2.4 years. That's more than $160,000 per average stay, according to the Federal Long-

Term Care Insurance Program, whose website (www.ltcfeds.com) has nursing home rate information for all 50 states.

Buying a policy in New York City with a $150 a day limit wouldn't cover half your costs, but in Des Moines, Iowa, it would be just about right. Obviously, it is less costly to cover your risk in Des Moines than in the Big Apple.

Benefit Period

Most insurance companies sell policies with a range of benefit periods, from two years to a lifetime. The longer you want to be covered the more you have to pay. Nearly 90 percent of those over age 65 who enter a nursing home stay fewer than five years. Your decision may be dictated by how much you can afford, but a policy with three or four years of coverage is a good bet. You have to decide what fits your budget and what lets you sleep at night. Because women generally live longer than men, they are more likely to have lengthier nursing home stays.

Waiting Period

The waiting period or "elimination period" is the time during which you must pay all the bills before the insurance kicks in. It is a deductible. Policies with longer waiting periods cost less than similar policies with shorter waits. Companies offer a range of elimination periods, from 20 days to a year. The Insurance Information Institute estimates that a policy with a 90-day waiting period costs about 30 percent less than one with a 30-day waiting period. But paying for those extra 60 days out-of-pocket would be costly. The 90-day option is popular, but make sure you can afford to pay for those first three months.

Inflation Protection

The average age of people admitted to nursing homes is 83. That means you could be holding a long-term care policy for two decades or more after your initial purchase. Over 20 years, nursing home charges go up considerably, and you need a benefit that keeps pace. Many policies offer at least two inflation protection options: five percent simple interest, or five percent compounded. It makes a big difference. At five percent simple interest, a $150-a-day benefit rises to $300 over 20 years. Compounding interest, the way inflation works in the real world, takes a $150 rate up to $398 over 20 years. Both options mean a higher premium, with the compounding feature costing more.

Other Policy Features

Look for policies that do the following:

- Let you stop paying premiums once you begin receiving benefits
- Cover Alzheimer's (must be diagnosed after purchasing policy)
- Allow you to downgrade coverage if you cannot afford the premiums
- Provide a discount if two spouses purchase coverage
- Are issued by solid companies with strong financial ratings

Policy Costs

The younger you are when you purchase a long-term care policy, the lower the price will be. And the premium does not automatically rise as you age. Prices can go up, but only for an entire class of policyholders. You cannot be singled out for a rate hike. Now that these policies have been around for 20 years or more, companies have learned to price them more effectively. In the early days, when

future liabilities were hard to estimate, many compan'
little and had to raise premiums. Experts say that is l
goes on.

One risk of waiting too long to apply for a policy is that you may
be turned down for health reasons. According to the Insurance Information Institute, if you apply in your fifties, there's a 1 in 10 chance
you'll be rejected. If you apply in your sixties, the chance of rejection
is 2 in 10. If you apply in your seventies, the chance of rejection is 4
in 10. The biggest factor, of course, is your health. If it is good, you
can probably get coverage.

Here are three hypothetical examples of policies and their prices.
All the policy applicants are in good health:

Man	**Woman**	**Man**
Age 57	Age 61	Age 66
Coverage: $130/day	Coverage: $100/day	Coverage: $100/day
Benefit period: 3 years	Benefit period: 3 years	Benefit period: 3 years
Waiting period: 90 days	Waiting period: 90 days	Waiting period: 90 days
Inflation: 5% compound	Inflation: 5% compound	Inflation: 5% simple
Annual premium: $1668	Annual premium: $1632	Annual premium: $1920

Depending on where these people live, they may need higher coverage limits, which would add to the premium. The sixty-six-year-old
man just has "simple interest" inflation protection. The compound
interest option would cost more. The National Association of Insurance Commissioners recommends that long-term care insurance premiums should not exceed seven percent of retirement income.

Tax Break (Maybe)

Premiums paid for long-term care insurance may be tax deductible, but only if you have sizable medical expenses. If you itemize deductions on Schedule A (Form 1040), you can deduct the amount of your total medical and dental expenses that exceed 7.5 percent of your adjusted gross income. Long-term care insurance premiums can be included as a medical expense, up to certain limits based on age (2006 amounts):

Age 40 or under	$280
Age 41 to 50	$530
Age 51 to 60	$1,060
Age 61 to 70	$2,830
Age 71 or over	$3,530

HEALTH CARE: THE BIG PICTURE

As we look ahead to our sixties, seventies, and beyond, Boomers have many options available to cover the costs of health care. But this combination of public and private insurance is costly and complex. The system also leaves behind millions of people who cannot afford the price of admission, or are denied coverage because of preexisting conditions. Health care expenses are rising much more rapidly than overall inflation or economic growth. This is putting a major strain on families, businesses, and governments. If our health care delivery system were a patient, the doctor would say, "You cannot keep this up. You need to slim down and shape up."

We look forward to longer lives and amazing breakthroughs in medical science. But all the miracle cures in the world won't help if we can't afford to pay for them.

Part Six

FAMILY AND COMMUNITY

14

FOUR GENERATIONS: BOOMERS ON POINT

Longer life spans and the complexity of modern life are rearranging some of our traditional family roles and responsibilities, and Boomers are at the center of these changes. Increasingly, families consist of four generations whose lives overlap for many years. The parents of Boomers are already enjoying a longevity bonus. In 1940, only about half (52 percent) of people age 50 still had a living parent. By 2000, that had increased to 80 percent. Back in 1940, 13 percent of sixty-year-olds had at least one living parent. By 2000, that had risen to 44 percent.

Many of today's seniors are living healthy, active lives and are quite capable of handling their affairs, thank you. But a large number will eventually face chronic illness. Cases of Alzheimer's are expected to rise substantially. Boomers will be handling many complex medical and financial issues for their parents. To a degree, this has always been true, but never to the level that is emerging today. The role of family manager and caregiver for an extended period is becoming a major responsibility at midlife, with considerable emotional and financial repercussions. And Boomers had better do this job well.

Their children are watching. It is projected that in 2050, more than 15 million Boomers will still be around. They will be 86 to 104 years old, and will be counting on help from their middle-aged (and older) children.

Speaking of those children, today's young adults have a harder time getting traction in their twenties. Education loans, high housing costs, expensive health care, credit card debt, and low paying entry-level jobs are all extending the time it takes to become independent adults. As a result, a large number of Boomer offspring rely on their parents for support well into their twenties.

Taking care of loved ones is what family is all about. But as Boomers face their own shortfalls in preparing for retirement, they have to avoid becoming overextended in meeting family needs. A friend of ours, a Boomer of modest means, recently helped his mom purchase a hearing aid, sent money to his daughter at college, and made a contribution to a grandchild's 529 college savings account. All wonderful causes, but he has to make sure he doesn't put his own financial security at risk.

In our public television series, Boomers! Redefining Life After Fifty (www.boomerstv.com), we profiled people who are experiencing firsthand the changing role of family, and three of those stories are included here. We met an artist who took dramatic action to help her parents in a medical crisis. We visited a couple who had not one, but two, boomerang kids move back home. And we heard the poignant story of empty nesters who suddenly had to take responsibility for parenting two young granddaughters. Four generations sharing many years together is a wonderful blessing, but it can also bring some challenges and heartache.

THE CERTAIN JOURNEY

Riki Moss is an artist in Somerville, Massachusetts. We met her during an exhibition of artwork by Boomers depicting the struggle of caring for elderly parents. The exhibit, shown at Somerville's Brickbottom Gallery, was called "The Certain Journey." Riki had contributed a large abstract mural to the showing. For Riki, an only child, and for her parents, the journey had become anything but certain.

"My parents were in Florida," says Riki. "They were 92 and 95, and living alone. They were pretending that everything was fine. I would go down and order catered meals and they would throw them out. I would get nursing care in there, and when I would call and ask about the nurses, they would say, 'Oh, they don't work for us anymore.'"

Riki's parents remained in their condo, but over time, the situation got worse. "Every time my mother had a medical emergency, my father would call 911, and the nurses would come back into the home and see that she couldn't deal with her medication. My father was trying. He thought he was taking care of her, but, in fact, he was killing her. He was giving her too much medication, or too little, and back in the hospital she would go."

Riki faced the wrenching question of whether to step in and take control. "I think this is hard for people to do. You have to understand that this is the moment when you need to take charge. I avoided it as long as I could. That was my relationship with my parents. It seemed very natural to allow them to run that show." But the "show" was stumbling, and eventually reached a crisis point. "The state of Florida called me up and said, 'We are going to take guardianship of your parents if you don't do something.'"

Riki got her parents into an assisted-living facility. She sold their condo. But medical issues persisted. "A year went by, they had another medical emergency, and they ended up in a nursing home. They hated it; we hated it. My father called the governor. He's a lawyer, he 'had his rights.' He wrote an article about elder abuse. He would just scream at me. And now and then he would get it, and he would be very grateful and thankful. And then I realized there was a lot of dementia going on, and he would go in and out."

After 14 trips to Florida within six months to check on her parents, Riki decided it was too much. "So I looked at them and said, 'Dad, that's it. I'm not coming down here anymore. If you want to see me you are going to have to move to Massachusetts.' And he said, 'Oh no, we're fine. We're just fine.'"

Finally, after her father had another medical setback, Riki went into action. "We got a guidance counselor. We got a lawyer. We got his legal team down there, doctors, the nursing people. We got them all together in a day, and we flew down. We got a Learjet. We got them slightly drugged and I told them, 'We are going to dinner.' And I put them on the plane. We arranged for a place here. It was great. There was a room for them together. And as soon as they got here, my father relaxed. He said, 'I don't have to do this anymore.' And he died within five months. And now she's there. She's not having a great life. I think this is really hard. She is not having any fun; she is miserable. And you know, there's not much you can do. Hospice is in there. Bereavement counseling is in there, but there is no memory, and it's tough."

Before her father's death, Riki had been working on her mural for the Brickbottom exhibition, but it had not really come together. She wasn't satisfied. The night he died, she went back into her studio and painted like mad. "I walked into the studio and I spent eight hours that night until dawn working on it. And it opened up in the most astonishing way. I was laughing and dancing. It's as if all this suffering had been released."

Riki is sad that she can't share her art with her ailing mother, but she did show her mom a photograph of the painting from the exhibition. "When she saw a picture of this painting, she said, 'Is that where I'm going?' It was a moment," says Riki. "It was a moment."

BOOMERS AND BOOMERANG KIDS

It's a beautiful summer afternoon and Judy Hanley is working the grill in the backyard of her modest suburban home. "It looks like we're eatin' great today," she says, as she flips one of four steaks sizzling on the grill. The steaks are for Judy, her husband Marty, and their two twenty-something sons, who live at home while paying off college loans and saving to buy homes of their own.

"I always say I live in a testosterone zone because I live with three males," says Judy. "The house is too small to cope with a lot of mess that comes along with four adults and all our gear."

Later, at the dinner table, Judy is kidding with her boys. "When you're living at home, it's kind of awkward," she says.

"It's actually awful living at home," says younger son Ryan. "Its such a turnoff to women, I find." Both boys are smart and good-looking. Turning off women does not appear to be a problem. "I'd love to buy a place because the interest rates are so low," says Ryan. "But you just can't afford anything around here."

At age 27, Patrick is a recent law school graduate, and owes about $100,000 in student loans. At the payment schedule he is on, he won't pay off the loans until he is 55. "I hope this doesn't mean you'll be living here 'til you're 55," chides Judy. Patrick doesn't miss a beat: "You guys will be long dead." Everyone laughs as Judy pretends to be stabbed in the heart.

"I knew that I would be able to move home, that my parents understood what I was doing," says Patrick. "They pushed me to get educated and they knew that they weren't going to pay for it, and I couldn't pay for it, and they supported me doing public interest work. So, as a result, I think they see it as sort of a joint venture."

When Patrick moved home, he joined Ryan who was already there saving to buy a condo. "Ryan never left," says Marty. "He went off to college and he came back."

"I consider myself very fortunate that my parents don't expect a rent check from me," says Ryan.

Actually, Judy wouldn't mind a rent check, but Marty takes a different view. "I remember paying a lot in my household, being from a large family," says Marty. "I worked two jobs. I know what it's like."

Judy considers her husband a soft touch. "Never the twain will meet on this topic, between Marty and I. We see it totally differently," she says. "I would like there to be some contribution to some of the household labor and more contribution perhaps toward a little rent.

Even if it's nominal. From ninth grade on, I always had to pay something into the household. I think there's a benefit to that."

"I always put money back into the household," says Marty. "But I didn't have a lot when I left. What I want them to do is have a lot when they leave, so they start off in life with something and go forward. They are here. It's a part of life. They're getting older and they're still my sons."

"Both of us are on the same page with wanting them to get ahead and be successful," adds Judy. "And if it means being home so that they can get ahead saving money, that's fine. They are a lot of fun and great guys, and very stimulating people and decent people, and so I think that's the best we've done. Raising a couple of good guys with good sets of values and a sense of spirit and fun and decency towards others. That for me is the cap."

"Yup," says Marty. "For me, too."

(GRAND) PARENTS IN A PINCH

While many Boomers are becoming empty nesters, some are taking on parenting roles all over again, with grandchildren. It happens for many reasons: illnesses, drug problems, accidental deaths. But an increasing number of parents are unable to care for their children. According to the 2000 Census, there are 2.3 million grandparents in the U.S. who are responsible for raising one or more of their grandchildren.

It's a responsibility that can arrive unexpectedly, as it did five years ago for Mary Pat Brittain and her husband Braxton, of Summerfield, North Carolina. "We had been empty nesters for eight years," says Mary. "We were entering the peak of our income when all of a sudden someone knocks on our door and we have a small baby and a child, and it completely turned our lives around."

According to Mary, her daughter, a single mother, had mental health problems and was not capable of raising her two little girls, Shannon, age 3, and Caroline, 14 months. The North Carolina Division of Social Services took custody of the girls and placed them with Mary and Braxton. Mary says it was a drastic change. "We had to pay for child care. We had to reorganize the house. We don't have the ability to pick up and go like we used to. That's probably the hardest part, that and our retirement dwindling because of the finances and everything. Like my husband said, you work all your life, you're focusing on what you are going to do when you retire, and you don't think you are going to be putting children through school and paying for weddings. It's just not anything you even think about."

Mary's daughter signed over her parental rights to the Brittains, and Mary and Braxton formally adopted the girls. "They have adapted quite well because they were in a situation where their needs were not met," says Mary. "It's got tons of rewards. When I get upset with my daughter because she is living a carefree life, I remember that she didn't see the first step. She doesn't get the hugs; she doesn't get the kisses and the giggles."

Mary had very clear advice for Boomers who are suddenly responsible for raising children. "I would say support groups are number one. That's what saved our bacon. We saw something in *Parade* magazine about AARP, and I went online and they told me about the GrandsPlace website (www.grandsplace.org). Those people told me about 'child only' grants. We had no idea that the girls could qualify for Medicaid and for child care. We went a whole year hitting our home equity to pay for child care. So I would tell people get a support group first and then find out what you can get for your children because it's the financial thing that puts people in a tailspin. A lot of the children come damaged and psychiatrists and psychologists cost a lot of money."

Aside from valuable advice, the support group helped to ease the feelings of isolation. "It's important to find people in the same situation as you are so you don't feel you are all alone. It's wonderful for the girls to be around other children that are also being raised by their grandparents. There's a lot of people out there like us, a lot of them."

RINKS AND DINKS

Many people do not have multiple generations to care for and rely upon. But single people and couples without children have many of their own financial planning needs. Ellen Siegel is a divorced midlife CFP from Miami whose practice is filled with Boomers who have no children.

"It seems that I resonate well with RINKS (Retired, Independent, No Kids) and DINKS (Double Income, No Kids). The issues that they face are different than Boomers with a younger generation to connect to and count on," says Siegel.

As Siegel began to realize how many emotional issues were attached to RINKS and DINKS and their money, she decided to team up with a therapist. They created an interactive program to help clients make financial decisions.

"We've created a Mindful Money workshop where we do psychodramas," says Siegel. "And we've seen some minimiracles with this approach. For example, I had a divorced woman client who was depressed and had given up. She hadn't even done her income taxes for five years! The workshops helped to get her 'unstuck.' Now her taxes are paid, she's sold her Florida home, and has moved out West. She's finally living the life she always dreamed about."

Mindful Money workshops cover traditional subjects like asset allocation and budgeting, but also include saying an abundance prayer. For clients who don't sign up for her workshops, Siegel regularly makes referrals to a therapist or life coach.

One growing Boomer scenario: middle-aged domestic partnerships. These involve unmarried couples, straight or gay, living together and mixing their finances.

"I see many couples who are different ages and who are at different life stages and this can cause issues. For example, one woman I see is in her early fifties and is finally working at her dream job. She's living with a guy sixty-two-years old who is retiring and wants to travel the world."

How does Siegel help these folks? Negotiation. "I don't talk about 'compromise.' I see that as a bad word . . . It means you're giving something up. 'Negotiate'—there's more power in this word. It means we each gain something," says Siegel.

Be Prepared

The issues and emotions around financial planning might be different when there are no children to be a support system for aging Boomers. But Siegel's mantra is the same for every one of her clients...get ready for the future!

"I operate my life on the Girl Scout motto: Be prepared!"

In her first meeting with new clients, Siegel takes a creative approach to getting to know them. Instead of asking for the budget first, she gives them paper and crayons. "I ask people to draw a family tree, including any pets. This gives me an instant picture of who else is involved in this financial plan. Most of us have significant others that we care for or rely upon. And pets are incredibly important. In fact, people who own parrots (birds that can live to be 90) have often already done estate planning for the bird!" says Siegel.

In their second meeting, Siegel asks, "What's on top right now? What's the big question, the number one goal? For many, it's, 'When can I stop working?' For others, it's, 'I might get downsized soon, what can I do to prepare?' Then we know what we have to begin to work toward."

Siegel says her clients are typically people like her: Boomers with an optimistic outlook on life but without children. "Having no kids puts a different psychological spin on how you look at your future. You might have plenty of money, a long-term care policy, and a fund to allow you to hire a driver if you can't drive. But who will be there when you get sick or have an operation?" That's a question Siegel always asks her single clients.

Siegel says good financial planning involves thinking about the social supports you need as you grow older. Who in your network do you call at 3 A.M. if you need help? "What I've seen over the years is that many of the strongest relationships my clients have are outside their bloodline," says Siegel. "I encourage people to formalize these social supports so they know who and what they can count on."

In spite of all the generational differences between Boomers and their parents, the two groups come to Siegel seeking the same ultimate financial goal: independence. The longevity revolution we're experiencing then becomes a challenge. When calculating how much money her clients will need to fund the rest of their lives, she uses age 99 for everyone unless there's a strong argument against that.

"The prospect of my forty-five- to fifty-year-old clients living 40 or 50 more years is a huge issue. We're not realizing how real that is yet," says Siegel.

15

AN ENCORE PERFORMANCE

If Boomers are going to enjoy a longevity bonus, should they share it with their neighbors? If we are going to have a long span of vitality after a primary career, will the social activism of our youth reassert itself through community service? If the answer is yes, Boomers have the potential to be a great force in tackling many of the nation's persistent social problems.

"They have an opportunity to give back," says author and columnist Abigail Trafford. "[Boomers] have been a privileged generation in terms of education and work and standard of living. I think many of them want to give back. We do want to be generous at this stage. We want to leave a legacy; we want people to know that we made a difference."

A 2004 study, "Reinventing Aging: Baby Boomers and Civic Engagement," by the Harvard School of Public Health and MetLife Foundation, concluded: "The baby Boomers soon will have the opportunity to redefine the meaning and purpose of the older years. As some of the demands of work and family that have commanded their attention in midlife recede, boomers will have the potential to become a social resource of unprecedented proportions by actively participating in the life of their communities."

Marc Freedman, cofounder of think tank and "innovation incubator" Civic Ventures, believes that the second half of life is a time for both individual and social renewal. Freedman calls this phenomenon "the experience dividend." However, he recognizes that not everyone is bullish on Boomers. "It's a bipartisan complaint—you've got people on the right like Pete Peterson who tell us that 'graying means paying,' that demography is disaster," says Freedman. "On the left, Lester Thurow's comment is that 'we've met the enemy and he is the elderly us.' So there seems to be one point that liberals and conservatives have managed to agree on these days and it's that this demographic revolution, this dramatic change in the population where 20 or 25 percent of the population is going to be over 60, is the worst thing that's ever happened to us."

It is true that sending monthly Social Security checks out to millions of Boomers, and paying their health care bills through Medicare, will be a huge financial drain on the country. But activists like Marc Freedman say the aging of America is as much an opportunity to be seized as a problem to be solved. "We're at the doorstep now of creating a new stage of life between the end of work and the end of people's health and well-being and independence," says Freedman. "We've got tens of thousands of people who are coming to a point where they've finished their midlife work, their job has run its course, the kids have moved out of the house, and yet they can look ahead at decades before they're going to be old. Yet they are unsure about what this period is about, what success is, what they should aspire to, even what to call themselves."

Freedman thinks many Boomers will be ready to answer the call to public service in programs such as Experience Corps (experiencecorps.org). Launched by Civic Ventures in the 1990s, Experience Corps matches older volunteers with elementary schools that need people to mentor and read to children. "The very generation that we created the Peace Corps for initially was now moving into their sixties," says Freedman. "We felt there was a good chance that they would have a second wind of activism." Experience Corps now operates in 20 cities. Many who work in the program are "pre-boomers," or members of the so-called Silent Generation, who have paved the way to a new vision of "retirement."

The Harvard MetLife study said this type of intergenerational program deserves special attention. "Studies have found that young people in such programs show measurable improvements in school attendance, attitudes toward school and the future, and attitudes toward elders. Adult volunteers report substantial benefits to themselves: the satisfaction of sharing their experience, feeling useful, and giving back to the community."

The study also called for an effort to motivate Boomers to deliver on their civic-minded intentions. "Although close to one-third of Boomers say they expect to participate in community service after retirement, there is a difference between intentions and actions, and Boomers may need a push. A national campaign—on a scale not previously attempted—might very well succeed in mobilizing Boomers to act on their stated intentions."

BOOMERS AND THE "HELPING" PROFESSIONS

Civic engagement means more than just volunteering. It can mean redirecting your paid work to address community needs. Studies have shown that a majority of Boomers plan to work past age 65, but that they want to work on their own terms. Many want to work part-time in new careers that have meaning and purpose. However, few researchers had asked, "What do these individuals actually want to do? What do they want to accomplish through work?" Civic Ventures conducted a survey of older adults to find out.

"We were stunned by the response to the study," says Marc Freedman. "Over half the people surveyed had interest in working in fields like education, human services, and health care. And within that, 21 percent of the Boomers in the survey said that they were extremely interested in doing this kind of work."

The emerging Boomer image of later life was the opposite of the old "golden years" vision. Instead of freedom *from* work, Boomers were looking for freedom *to* work.

Freedman points out that the Boomers have four times the high school and college graduation rates of the previous generation. There is currently a shortage of teachers, nurses, and managers for the non-profit sector. But will Boomers be recruited for and welcomed into these professions?

"The nonprofit sector is in the midst of a leadership crisis long on idealism, short on experience," says Freedman. "Places like Wal-Mart and Home Depot are doing a much better job reaching out to this population than the nonprofit sector is, than education is, and I think that we're going to need to wake up if we have any chance of making the most of these developments," says Freedman. "I think we have to devise a compelling marketing campaign to capture the time, talent, hearts, minds, experience, and interest of this population and I think that we've yet to do that."

"Let's begin to balance opportunity for productivity, engagement, and purpose across the life span," says Freedman. "One of the things we learned in our survey is that it isn't primarily idealism that drives people. It's two other, more immediate desires: the need for purpose, a reason to get up in the morning; and people, connection to other people."

MANY WAYS TO SERVE

Boomers can "give back" in many ways, with time, money, and expertise. Areas with the greatest need are at the two ends of the age spectrum, young and old. Similar to Experience Corps, the Big Brother and Big Sister programs connect men and women volunteers with children who need an adult's guiding hand. The program always has a long waiting list of children. Youth athletic leagues, scouting programs, arts organizations, and social service groups are fueled by volunteers who make a significant contribution to the community.

Hospitals rely on volunteers to direct visitors and spend time with patients.

The civic engagement study from Harvard and MetLife found that existing charitable institutions may need to be revamped to absorb Boomer volunteers and make the most of their interests and preferences. "Many local agencies will not have the resources for professional volunteer management, so new mediating institutions, or third parties, may be needed to handle recruitment, training, and referral of Boomers."

The federally funded Senior Corps connects people 55 and up with individuals and organizations that need assistance (www.seniorcorps.gov). Programs include the following:

- **Foster Grandparent Program:** Volunteers ages 60+ mentor, support, and help some of the most vulnerable children in the U.S.
- **Senior Companion Program:** Brings together volunteers ages 60 and over with adults in their community who have difficulty with the simple tasks of daily living. Companions assist with shopping and light chores, interacting with doctors, or just making a friendly visit.
- **RSVP:** Connects volunteers age 55 and up with service opportunities in their communities that match their skills and availability. RSVP volunteers provide hundreds of community services, such as these:
  - Tutoring children in reading and math
  - Building houses
  - Helping get children immunized
  - Modeling parenting skills to teen parents
  - Participating in neighborhood watch programs
  - Planting community gardens
  - Providing counsel to new business owners
  - Offering relief services to victims of natural disasters
  - Helping community organizations operate more efficiently

Some Boomers may prefer opportunities for civic engagement that do not involve working through an established group. Friends and neighbors can organize a community clean-up day. A family can check in on an elderly neighbor. Residents on a block can organize a tag sale to raise funds for a local charity. Informal initiatives should be encouraged and valued as alternatives to agency-based volunteer service.

In our public television series on Boomers, we did profiles of several people who are giving back in a variety of ways, and we include three of those stories here. We meet a retired executive who uses his business skills to help a community farm. We learn how a group of women has created a "giving circle" to pool their charitable contributions. And we travel to Puerto Rico with a veterinarian who provides medical care for local animals as part of his Caribbean vacation.

AN EXPERIENCED FARMHAND

Bill Huss is in the barnyard of the Codman Community Farm in Lincoln, Massachusetts, trying to herd some pigs back into their pen. The pigs are running around, oinking and squealing, and Bill looks up and says, "It's a humbling experience. You realize there are no rank and privileges when you are dealing with farm animals."

Bill's mother was from Ohio, where her family has had a farm since the 1800s. Though farming is in his roots, his career was in energy services and conservation. He was able to retire from the company in his mid-fifties, a few years after it was bought out. At about the same time his mother passed away. "So I no longer have any parents, and that gives you a sense that life is finite," says Bill. "So, with all of that coming together, here's an opportunity to do something else. There's only so many years to do what is really important, so I decided to take the plunge and do some of the things that I had been thinking about."

Bill volunteers at the Codman Community Farm, where he serves on the board, does farm chores, and helps the farm with its business operations. The nonprofit farm, which makes money selling hay, provides educational opportunities for children to learn about agriculture, and it preserves 130 acres of suburban land from being developed. Bill also volunteers as a Big Brother, and teaches part-time at Babson College.

"I don't even like using the term retirement any more. In a way, it's a career change, a lifestyle change. It's freedom, it's flexibility. It's saying, 'How can I make my life worthwhile over the next years?'"

Like many in the first wave of Boomers, Bill's values were shaped by the turbulent times of the late '60s and early '70s. "I think the most influential factor in my life was the time that I went to college. I was in college in the early 1970s and that was right at the tail end of a lot of social consciousness-raising and activism, whether it be the Vietnam War or the war on poverty or civil rights. There were a lot of college students who were very interested in trying to make things better."

In forging a new life following his primary career, Bill has reconnected to the idealism of his youth. "As many people in my generation, I got away from that to some extent. I had a career in energy conservation and the environment, which made me feel good. But I also wanted to progress in my career and make money, and do all the things that pulled me away from some of the ideals that I had lived with in my college years, so I really wanted to get back to that."

Bill Huss is grateful that he was able to "retire" at an early age and have the opportunity to keep working, but on his own terms. "I still go out to the golf course, and take some nice vacations, but that doesn't give me fulfillment. That's relaxing, but it doesn't give me the feeling that I'm able to contribute something that I've gained through years of working. I'm just as active as when I was working but I don't have to worry about a boss, a paycheck, or the stress of managing a business. I can now focus on things that contribute to community and make me feel good about what I'm doing in the world."

GIVING CIRCLE

When Susan Priem went to graduate school in midlife, she attended the Kennedy School of Government at Harvard University and studied philanthropy. She was surprised to learn that women, even wealthy women, are reluctant to donate large amounts of money to charity. She wondered how to change that and started to talk to her friends about their style of giving.

What she discovered is that women like to give "in connection." The act of getting together in a social setting, doing research together, talking things over, making plans in a group...this process was as valuable to women as the act of writing a check.

"I was surprised at how many women wanted to join a group, to act together in person rather than sit at home alone and make a donation," says Priem. She formed what is known as a "giving circle" in the western suburbs of Boston. About 20 women got together that first year, set down some basic principles and called themselves the Hestia Fund, after the Greek goddess of the hearth.

"We decided that we would always show respect to each other at every meeting," said Priem. "We also decided that we would each give the same amount of money each month and that we would make a multiyear commitment."

The Hestia Fund's members donate $5,000 a year each for three years. In addition to the money, most join a committee and donate a lot of time. A grants committee finds and talks to potential nonprofit partners who are looking for funds, makes site visits, and finally makes a recommendation to the group on which organizations they want to fund.

"We decided to support charities that benefit women and their children," says Linda Nelson, now president of the Fund, which has grown to more than 50 members in six years. "All of us had been involved with our children's school activities and with nonprofits over the years. But now that we're in our fifties and our kids are grown, we needed a way to stay together, working for a good cause. The Fund helps us do that."

One nonprofit in East Boston that benefits from the Hestia Fund's involvement is Zumix, an after-school music education program for children, many of them from immigrant families. The Fund subsidizes individual music lessons, musical instruments, and even a radio station.

"When I go to Zumix and see what the students are doing, hear the music and meet their parents, I get a real 'gut feeling' for the organization," says Hestia Fund member Victoria Croll. "We do real due diligence and we can see the difference that our funding can make in the lives of very talented young people. It's very rewarding."

Susan Priem says they will keep the Hestia Fund relatively small to keep the sense of community, to be able to meet in one person's living room each month and really connect with each other personally. But they plan to help grow the concept of giving circles by meeting with other women interested in the concept.

"Our goal is to increase the involvement of women in philanthropy," says Priem, "not to make Hestia Fund a big organization."

Giving circles are growing in popularity, with more than 255 nationally and more than $44 million donated to various causes. Even though the Hestia Fund has given away more than $1 million in grants in the Greater Boston area, for these Boomers, it isn't all about the money.

"The social aspect of getting together in community is just as important as the charity itself," says Linda Nelson. "Women like to stay connected to each other and doing so with a purpose makes it all that much more rewarding."

VACATIONING VET

For the past 12 years, fifty-one-year-old John Kelley has been spending weeks at a time on the island of Vieques, Puerto Rico. "The first thing a lot of people on this island learn is that you have to drive defensively," says Kelley. "Not so much the other cars, but the horses or cows that you might run into."

John first visited the island as a tourist in the early '90s. The Caribbean sun and beautiful vistas were the attraction the first time around. But what kept John coming back was the island's forgotten population, the animals. Kelley has been practicing veterinary medicine for 21 years. Back home on Cape Cod, he owns an animal hospital and operates three clinics. On Vieques, Kelley inspects dogs with distended bellies, and horses with eye infections, and he does it all for free.

"The first time I came here was for fun to see the island. But once I got here and did a little bit of work, it became a little more than that. This island over the last 12 years has become a working vacation, but it doesn't really seem like work."

"He's considered a volunteer vacationer, if there is such a thing," says Barbara Rumore, who heads the board at the Humane Society of Vieques, a nonprofit organization run by volunteers. "We have contract vets and they charge $300 a day," says Barbara. "So when John comes, that's $300 that can be spent on medicines, food, telephones, lights, water."

The mission of the Humane Society is relatively new to Vieques. Until Kelley and others like him took charge, the island was home to an abundance of stray animals with no official plans for sterilization. "The first time I came here, there were lots of dogs, they had no owners. They just lived off trash from the different restaurants."

Island life is a change of pace for John, and practicing veterinary medicine on Vieques is hardly routine. "Here, it's still back 30 years ago. There's no X-ray machine. There's no ultrasound machine. But it makes it fun. For lack of a better word, it's cowboy medicine. You have to fly by the seat of your pants."

When he goes to Vieques, John has a great vacation, but he comes home with more than just a suntan and a few postcards. "I can give something back to this island," he says. "I'm not just a tourist. I'm not just a person eating in the restaurants here, or laying on the beach. I really feel like I'm doing something for the people and the animals, and that's a good feeling, too. So you go home relaxed and feeling good about yourself. You can't ask for much more than that. And I don't."

HERE'S TO YOUR HEALTH

Several scientific studies indicate a link between volunteer activity and better health as people age. The science is not definitive, but experts suggest a number of reasons why giving of ourselves can be beneficial. People who volunteer are less isolated. They build new social connections, which can improve mental health. While doing work aligned with their interests, they continue to learn and to enjoy personally rewarding experiences. In sharing their knowledge and skills, and in seeing the results of their efforts, volunteers enjoy enhanced self-esteem. Making a contribution provides meaning in life, and that is true at any age. If we Boomers are fortunate enough to have the time, health, energy, and resources to help others, we can go a long way in making life better for our fellow citizens, and for ourselves.

Books Cited in the Text

Fred Brock *Retire on Less Than You Think: The New York Times Guide to Planning Your Financial Future* **Times Books, 2004**

Fred Brock *Health Care on Less Than You Think: The New York Times Guide to Getting Affordable Coverage* **Times Books, 2006**

George Kinder *The Seven Stages of Money Maturity* **Delacorte Press, 1999**

Jonathan Pond *You Can Do It! The Boomer's Guide to a Great Retirement* **Collins, 2007**

Jeri Sedlar and Rick Miners *Don't Retire, Rewire!: 5 Steps to Fulfilling Work That Fuels Your Passion, Suits Your Personality, or Fills Your Pocket* **Alpha, 2002**

Abigail Trafford *My Time: Making the Most of the Bonus Decades After 50* **Basic Books, 2004**

Additional Recommended Reading

Mitch Anthony *The New Retirementality* **Kaplan, 2001**

Richard Nelson Bolles *What Color Is Your Parachute? 2007: A Practical Manual for Job-Hunters and Career-Changers* **Ten Speed Press, 2006**

Ken Dychtwald, Tamara Erickson, Robert Morison *Workforce Crisis: How to Beat the Coming Shortage of Skills and Talent* **Harvard Business School Press, 2006**

Marc Freedman *Prime Time: How Baby Boomers Will Revolutionize Retirement and Transform America* **Public Affairs, 2002**

Dee Lee *Women and Money: Your Personal Finance Guide* **Flying Pig Publishing, 2003**